EMPOWER YOUR SELF-ESTEEM

NURTURE YOUR SELF-WORTH, BUILD EMOTIONAL RESILIENCE, AND CULTIVATE LASTING JOY WITH THE POWER OF POSITIVE SELF-TALK

SCOTT ALLAN

Empower Your Self-Esteem

Nurture Your Self-Worth, Build Emotional Resilience, and Cultivate Lasting Joy with the Power of Positive Self-Talk

More Bestselling Titles From Scott Allan

Empower Your Thoughts

Drive Your Destiny

Relaunch Your Life

The Discipline of Masters

Do the Hard Things First

Undefeated

No Punches Pulled

Fail Big

Rejection Free

Built for Stealth

Check out the complete collection of books and training here:

www.scottallanbooks.com

Empower Your
Self-Esteem

*Nurture Your **Self-Worth**, Build **Emotional Resilience**, and Cultivate **Lasting Joy** with the Power of **Positive Self-Talk***

By Scott Allan

Scott Allan
PUBLISHING S A
ONE BOOK AT A TIME

Copyright page

JOIN THE COMMUNITY OF 30,000 LIFETIME LEARNERS!

Sign up today for my **free weekly newsletter** and receive instant access to **the <u>onboarding subscriber pack</u>** that includes:

The Fearless Confidence Action Guide: 9 Action Plans for Building Limitless Confidence and Achieving Sustainable Results!

The bestseller poster pack: A poster set of Scott Allan's bestselling books

The Zero Procrastination Blueprint: A Step-by-Step Blueprint to Turn Procrastination into Rapid Action Implementation!

Begin Your Journey and Make This Life Your Own. Click Here to <u>Subscribe Today</u>, or scan the <u>QR code</u> below.

CONTENTS

"It is an absolute human certainty that no one can know his own beauty or perceive a sense of his own worth until it has been reflected back to him in the mirror of another loving, caring human being."

— **John Joseph Powell,** *The Secret of Staying in Love*

Introduction: Empower Your Self-Esteem

"Self-esteem is a powerful force within each of us... Self-esteem is the experience that we are appropriate to life and the requirements of life."

Nathaniel Branden

NOTE TO MY READERS: This book has the power to be a powerful beacon of positivity and transformation in your life by simply helping you realize and nurture your self-worth. Use it well to begin the journey to unlocking your true power.

If you are reading this book, it is because you either have a low sense of self-worth or struggle with rebuilding and maintaining healthy self-esteem.

I want you to know that it is okay to feel that way. You are not alone on this journey. That said, you have the power to feel better and to be better in all ways, and with this guide, I am committed to helping you achieve that.

As you read through this book, you will realize that self-esteem is vital to living a happy, fulfilling, and balanced life.

Quite often, we complain about how our life isn't good enough, how we struggle to find peace of mind, or how others are doing well while we feel and seem stuck where we were years ago.

If you dig deeper into these issues to find the root cause, you will discover that the problem comes from not feeling worthy enough. When we don't like ourselves or who we are, we find problems in everything, even everyone around us.

We cannot pursue our passions, follow through with our goals, do things that bring us joy, and feel peaceful because, deep down, we just aren't happy with ourselves.

A negative self-view is a serious issue because how you see and value yourself significantly affects your mood, feelings, mindset, attitude, behavior, and actions. Well, simply put, it influences your entire life. So, it is something that needs your utmost attention.

But first, let me ask you this... What do you think of when you hear the word "self-esteem"?

I'm sure we all have an idea of what this means. Simply stated, it is what we think, feel and believe about ourselves. However, it really isn't as simple as that. An important thing to know is that there are many factors that influence self-esteem at any given time in your life and it can fluctuate throughout your lifetime.

"Self-esteem" is composed of the thoughts, feelings, and beliefs we hold about ourselves. Since our thoughts, feelings, and beliefs change constantly, our self-esteem is continually evolving. Having low self-esteem can harm your mental health, relationships, and school or career life. However, there are several ways to feel better about yourself and boost your self-esteem.

The things that lower our self-esteem can be different for everyone. Difficult life experiences can typically be a factor, such as abuse as a child or an adult, relationship problems, financial issues, or physical health problems. Also, how you treat yourself can influence your self-esteem, such as how you talk to yourself (self-talk), criticizing yourself, and seeing yourself as "not important"

In this book—Empower Your Self-Esteem— I will teach you the greatest ways to raise your self-esteem so that you are feeling absolutely great and with limitless potential in your life. As a result of following through and building self-esteem in your life, you will begin to feel better, look better, and respond better to your environment and in relationships.

With this book, you have the power to build your self-esteem, but you need guidance, a gentle nudge, and inner motivation to stay true to this path.

This "gentle nudge" is precisely where this guide serves its purpose. It is a consciously crafted blueprint that aims to help you understand self-esteem. It provides actionable, clearly explained, easy-to-follow guidelines and strategies to build and grow your self-esteem and empower you.

Here is what you will discover in this book:

- ✓ An evaluation of the self-esteem spectrum

- ✓ The difference between narcissism and self-esteem

✓ The Importance of self-esteem on mental health, physical well-being, work, productivity, relationships, success, and life in general

✓ Low self-esteem and, how its vicious cycle affects your life

✓ The different myths surrounding self-esteem

✓ How positive self-talk builds and boosts your self-esteem

✓ The significance of self-love, what it truly means, and how to nurture it

✓ Why you need to embrace your individuality and how to do it

✓ Constructive ways to handle criticism without hurting your self-esteem

✓ The mind-body connection and its effect on self-esteem

✓ How mindfulness is a powerful tool in fostering self-esteem

✓ Strategies to cultivate mindfulness to augment your self-worth

✓ The link between stress and self-esteem and positive ways to manage stress

✓ The importance of healthy relationships on your self-worth

✓ Strategies to distinguish between toxic and healthy relationships and how to break the former while cultivating the latter

✓ Self-esteem and reclaiming your inner power

✓ The power of goal setting, along with strategies to set and objectify your meaningful goals

✓ Why you need to adopt a lifelong learning attitude and how to do it

✓ The important role of creativity in shaping your self-worth

✓ The power of gratitude, its relation to self-esteem, and strategies to become more grateful

✓ Why and how to empower others to improve your self-worth

✓ Spirituality and its role in the self-esteem equation

✓ The need to heal past wounds along with actionable ways to do so

✓ The true meaning of resilience, its relation to self-esteem, and ways to become more resilient

✓ How to monitor your performance, learn from setbacks, and journey through life while becoming better every day

You will find all these aspects covered in the different chapters of this book, which I wrote with a lot of love, care, and experience. I have endeavored to write every chapter in a manner that educates you about the concept covered in it and then takes you on a step-by-step journey to implement it in your life.

For instance, if you are in the chapter about mindfulness and self-esteem, I will walk you through mindfulness and its beautiful relationship with self-esteem, so you understand the need to become more mindful. Following that, you will learn simple but amazingly powerful strategies that help make mindfulness a daily part of your life.

All the chapters are interconnected to ensure everything flows seamlessly, but you can skip to the most relevant chapter based on your circumstances. For example, if you have time constraints and need to focus more on building healthy relationships to grow your self-esteem, you can skim through the initial chapters or skip them and jump right to the one centered on relationships.

Overall, this book can provide you with a comprehensive understanding of self-esteem and offer practical and actionable advice for improving your self-esteem and living a happier, more fulfilling life.

Let's get started with the journey. Before moving on, please read the following sentence and say it aloud five times.

"I am the measure of my worth, and I say I am worthy."

Go on—repeat it five times loudly.

Now, take a deep breath and tune into how you feel. You are feeling a tad bit better than before, right? Be honest, please. Even if you feel the same, acknowledge that. At least you are not feeling worse. If you keep repeating this sentence, you will start feeling good because this affirmation breathes self-esteem into you.

Whether you struggle with low self-esteem or simply want to boost your confidence and self-worth, this book offers practical and actionable advice for improving your self-esteem and living a happier, more fulfilling life.

With the understanding that you alone determine your self-worth, let us move on and begin the greatest training you have ever invested in.

I hope you enjoy this book, and learn how to build unbreakable self-esteem in your life from today to last a lifetime!

Scott Allan

www.scottallanbooks.com

Chapter 1: Unraveling the Essence of Self-Esteem

"No one can make you feel inferior without your consent."

Eleanor Roosevelt

A big reason many of us don't work on our self-esteem is because we don't really understand it. Most of us do not learn it in school and have no other way to learn about it. Also, many of us didn't hear talks or discussions about this important aspect when we were growing up.

As sad as this reality is, it's never too late to learn, so let's start with the basics. In this opening chapter, we'll delve into self-esteem to demystify its nature and distinguish it from closely related terms such as self-confidence and narcissism.

By the end of this chapter, you will have a good understanding of the basic aspects of self-esteem.

But first, *what is self-esteem?*

Self-esteem is more than just a buzzword; it's a fundamental element of our psyche that shapes our daily lives. When you think of self-esteem, think of it as the lens through which you see yourself. The internal narrative whispers encouragement or criticism, guiding your actions, reactions, and decisions.

At its core, self-esteem is about self-perception. It is how you value yourself, both internally and in relation to the world around you. For example, saying things like "I feel good about myself," "I don't like myself," "I know I can do this," and "I'll never get through the problems in my life" reflect your self-esteem.

Think of self-esteem as your inner compass. When properly calibrated, it points you toward self-knowledge and guides you toward understanding your worth and abilities. This inner voice tells you, "You can do this," or "You are enough," even when faced with challenges.

Please understand that healthy self-esteem is not about believing you're above others. It is about recognizing your unique value and not allowing yourself to be undervalued or mistreated.

On the other hand, if your self-esteem is low, this compass can lead you astray. You may find yourself constantly battling self-doubt, questioning your decisions, or being overly critical of your actions. It is okay to criticize yourself from time to time. I mean, we've all gone through times when things have taken a turn for the worse and we ended up saying, "Man, I never do things the right way.

However, if this feeling persists, and you question your value and your ability to do things well in almost everything, and you are overly critical of yourself, you are only demeaning yourself. This persistent self-criticism isn't just a passing phase. It can become a significant obstacle to your progress in various facets of your life, whether personal, professional, or social.

Self-esteem is important to understand because it is dynamic, not static. It fluctuates based on experience, feedback, and internal dialogue. However, with awareness and conscious effort, you can nurture and maintain a healthy level of self-esteem, ensuring that it serves as a positive force in your life.

But what shapes this sense of self? Many factors come into play, from past experiences and personal accomplishments to societal norms and cultural influences.

Our environment, the media we watch, the people we meet, and the interactions we have all shape how we perceive ourselves. In addition, our societies have set different benchmarks for worthiness, success, adequacy, and happiness. When we fall short of these benchmarks, we feel inadequate, which affects our self-esteem.

Self-esteem has two very important components: self-love and self-competence. To understand the true nature of self-esteem and then to build it, it is crucial to understand these two elements:

The Two Components of Self-Esteem

Your self-esteem comes from loving yourself and feeling adequate, or better known as self-competence.

Let's get a better understanding of these two concepts.

Self-Competence

Self-competence refers to an inner sense of competence and adequacy. It means that you feel competent and know that you can do the things you want to do. Competence is related to feeling motivated. When you feel motivated to achieve a goal, you are willing to go the extra mile to fight and overcome the obstacles that come your way.

To value yourself, you need to work on feeling competent enough. This feeling comes from doing things you enjoy, not giving up in the face of adversity, and having a can-do attitude.

Self-love

Self-love refers to accepting yourself as you are and then cultivating a sense of love for yourself. Now don't get me wrong. Self-love does not mean bragging about your shortcomings while resisting self-improvement and evolution.

It is simply being kind to yourself, understanding that you are human and therefore prone to error, and that being imperfect is okay. Instead of belittling yourself for your shortcomings and bad habits such as smoking, procrastination, temper problems, and the like, you accept them as part of your healthy experience as a human being and understand that you need to work on your not-so-good qualities while being kind to yourself.

The ability to love yourself gives you the strength to have compassion for yourself when the going gets tough. Instead of succumbing to the pressures and challenges you face, you calm yourself and find the courage to get back up and try again. As you continue to battle your problems, you continue to cultivate self-competence. Together, self-love and self-competence pave the way for healthy self-esteem.

As mentioned earlier, when you have healthy self-esteem, you love yourself and are proud of yourself.

Now, many people may confuse this with narcissism. So let us look at narcissism and how it differs from having healthy self-esteem.

Improving How You Feel About Yourself

People who experience a steady diet of disapproval from important others-family, bosses, friends, teachers-may have feelings of low self-esteem. However, the healthy individual is able to withstand discouraging evaluations.

Each person's experience is different, but over the course of a lifetime, self-esteem seems to rise and fall in a predictable, systematic way. Research suggests that self-esteem increases to varying degrees until age 60, when it remains stable, before beginning to decline in old age.

Self-esteem can affect life in many ways, from academic and career success to relationships and mental health. However, self-esteem is not an immutable trait; successes or setbacks, both personal and professional, can cause fluctuations in self-esteem.

Self-esteem vs. narcissism: Understanding the Differences

Self-esteem is your evaluation of yourself. High self-esteem means that you value yourself while accepting and working on your shortcomings. Narcissism, on the other hand, is when your ego becomes so inflated that you become self-centered and believe you are superior to others.

Loving and accepting yourself does not make you selfish and self-centered. It only makes you kinder to yourself so that you can love yourself and work to improve yourself, even when you do things you are not proud of. You understand that you have problems to deal with, and you do so without being mean and unkind to yourself.

However, if you have narcissistic tendencies, you tend to ignore your flaws and negative qualities altogether. It does not matter if your negativity hurts others because you focus only on what makes you feel good about yourself.

This creates an inflated ego that gives you a sense of superiority. You don't think anyone is right or can correct you, so narcissism is an emotional issue that requires serious attention.

The path to self-esteem

Now that you understand the basic concept of self-esteem, you are ready to begin the journey of building your self-esteem. As you begin this journey, it is important to understand that it is not about reaching a fixed end point, but about embracing the continuous process of self-discovery and growth.

The truth is that your self-esteem can never reach a fixed end point because our lives and personalities are constantly evolving. Everything we go through shapes our perceptions and how we value ourselves. Many of us experience more setbacks than others. To ensure that these setbacks don't demoralize us, we need to constantly work on our self-esteem, which is why I refer to "building your self-esteem" as an ongoing process.

I have designed this book to be your trusted companion on this journey. Think of it as a map, charting the terrain of self-esteem, highlighting potential pitfalls, and illuminating the way with proven strategies. It is here to offer insights that debunk common misconceptions about self-esteem to ensure that the myths or misconceptions do not lead you astray.

From harnessing the transformative power of positive affirmations to using visualization, I have designed each chapter to equip you with practical techniques. These aren't just theoretical concepts; they're actionable strategies proven to make a tangible difference.

Every step of the way, this guide will be right beside you, guiding, encouraging, and celebrating your milestones. Together, we'll navigate the complex landscape of self-esteem to ensure that you emerge empowered, confident, and ready to embrace life's myriad opportunities.

As you've journeyed through this chapter, you've taken the first steps toward a deeper exploration of self-esteem. Now, let's take it a step further and talk in detail about how self-esteem affects the different areas of our lives.

Chapter 2: The Importance of Self-Esteem

"Self-esteem is crucial to how much or how little contentment you feel at the end of your life."

Mark Goulston

I n the previous chapter, we established that self-esteem forms the basis for how we perceive ourselves and crucially shapes our interactions with the outside world.

Let us now take a closer look at how high and low self-esteem affects and shapes the various aspects of our lives.

The impact on our life choices

Many years ago, in high school, I wanted to participate in a debate competition. I even had the whole debate ready in my head. But whenever I thought about signing up, I often talked myself out of it. The reason? I was sure that I would suck at it. Why did I feel that way?

It was because I thought I was not good enough, even though I had practiced and gone over the points I would argue. I did not feel good about myself, so I had low self-esteem. I did not enter this competition or pursue many of my passions for quite some time simply because of my low self-esteem.

When you feel good about yourself, you know that you are good enough to do anything you want. Even if you think you might not be good at something or have the skills to try or excel at it, you know you can at least try, practice, and improve. If I had healthy self-esteem when I wanted to enter that debate tournament, I would have at least entered.

High self-esteem gives you the courage to believe in yourself, even when things don't seem to be going your way. You know that nothing is the end of the world, and you feel confident in making decisions based on your wants and needs. You can decide to pursue a career in architecture, learn a new language, take tap dancing lessons, go backpacking in Western Europe, or do anything you want.

Taking risks and facing challenges also becomes easy when you have healthy self-esteem. Yes, taking risks and facing problems are also important life choices.

Growth is not easy. It requires you to step out of your comfort zone, to be a little uncomfortable for a while, and to embrace challenging times. That's when you transform into your warrior self and grow by leaps and bounds.

Whether it's starting a business, shifting gears in your career, taking a break from work and going on a journey of self-exploration, or ending a toxic relationship and moving on to a healthier one, you feel strong enough to make such decisions when your self-esteem is high.

The role self-esteem plays in our relationships

Just as self-esteem has a major impact on your life choices, it also has a major impact on your relationships. The best relationships have a foundation of love, respect, caring, trust, empathy, and faith. So where does self-esteem fit into this equation?

You may have seen many roles and memes about how "you can't pour from an empty cup. Well, that's 100% true. If a cup is empty, it will not pour anything. Similarly, if you don't have love, respect, empathy, and trust for yourself, you can't pour it out to your loved ones, be they your parents, siblings, partner, children, friends, or anyone else.

Not only that, but you are likely to constantly doubt yourself and rely more on others in various relationships to make your own decisions. Perhaps your father makes all your decisions for you, or you always look to your partner to make your career choices; this may seem okay on the surface, but deep down it affects how you feel about yourself, and your self-confidence continues to erode.

Also, you are likely to become a pushover if you cannot think for yourself, make personal decisions, and stand up for yourself. If your coworkers often dump their piles of work on you while you feel helpless but cannot muster the courage to speak up, you know what I am talking about.

If you have low self-esteem, you will always doubt yourself. You are also likely to value and admire others more and feel indebted to them for even being around you. This feeling makes you vulnerable to unhealthy behaviors, such as giving in to whatever a loved one or authority figure wants.

For example, your partner may have a habit of yelling at you, and although you disapprove of this behavior, you are afraid to bring up the issue with them. Because you devalue yourself, you are likely to see them as the more assertive person who deserves respect. As a result, you succumb to their mistreatment.

Conversely, things change for the better when you have healthy self-esteem. High self-esteem makes you understand and accept that you deserve love, care, and respect.

You know you are not perfect (who is, really?), but you know you are not worthy of abuse and mistreatment. Because you respect yourself, you set the right standard for others to treat you the right way.

Let's continue with the earlier example of the yelling partner. If you have healthy self-esteem, you will not accept this unhealthy behavior. So when your partner yells at you, you will have the courage to confront them, let them know how upset you are, and set the boundary for them to treat you with more respect.

With the ability to set healthy boundaries, you can successfully maintain healthy and happy relationships and avoid the toxic ones that can eat away at your well-being.

In addition, when you love and value yourself, you take better care of yourself; this allows you to better focus on building happier and more fulfilling relationships with your loved ones.

When you have a healthy and stable state of mind, you find it easier to listen to your loved ones' problems and even help them solve them. You will also be able to control your emotions in volatile situations and maintain the peace that further strengthens your bond.

The gist of this discussion is that a high sense of self-worth contributes positively and massively to building happier and more meaningful relationships, so you surround yourself with people who truly matter and make you happy.

The impact on career and success

Imagine you have come across a great career opportunity that allows you to move to the country of your dreams, earn a six-figure salary, and enjoy tremendous growth. It is okay to feel a little scared and even overwhelmed by this offer.

However, if you have a healthy self-esteem, you will probably accept the offer because you believe in yourself that you can do this job successfully and transition happily to the new place; this is the power of building your self-esteem. It makes you believe in yourself completely and focus on growth and improvement. You find the courage to take risks, experiment with things, focus on learning, and keep moving up the ladder of success (however you define success).

Conversely, when your self-esteem is low, you hold yourself back from reaching your full potential. You are more afraid of failure and setbacks because you believe you are incompetent and likely to make a fool of yourself in a challenging situation.

You also believe that you will never be able to be proud of yourself because you don't have it in you to reach milestones. As bizarre as it sounds, low self-esteem makes you feel this way.

But the good news is, it doesn't have to be that way. You have this blueprint for boosting your self-esteem. If you continue to follow the strategies while believing in yourself completely, you will emerge as a victorious warrior who knows you can do anything you want.

The Emotional Health Footprint

Our quality of life is directly proportional to our emotional well-being. Fortunately, this topic has been the subject of much discussion and emphasis over the past decade. However, it still needs further discussion because we often ignore our emotional health without realizing how it affects our lives.

When we are emotionally healthy, we can better focus on every aspect of our lives, whether it is our personal well-being, self-improvement, relationships, work, career, growth, spirituality, or financial matters.

To accomplish this, we must first pay attention to building our self-esteem. Emotional problems such as anxiety, chronic stress, and depression often accompany low self-esteem.

When you constantly put yourself down, you tend to feel hopeless and worthless; this often triggers a never-ending loop of negative thoughts that continue to pull you down. You are your own biggest cheerleader; if you do not cheer for yourself, chances are that no one else will.

Low self-esteem also makes you more susceptible to criticism, and you are more likely to succumb to the negativity of any harsh comment that comes your way, rather than use it constructively. You also tend to see the criticism as confirmation of your inadequacy, which only weakens your self-confidence.

High self-esteem is a buffer against emotional problems. Because you know that adversity isn't permanent, you find the inner strength to get through tough times with your head held high. Although you sometimes feel stressed, you know how to deal with it positively and not let it affect your emotional health. You bounce back from rough patches because you have faith in your abilities and know that 'this too shall pass'.

In addition, healthy self-esteem instills in you the belief that you are amazing and can overcome and improve upon all your shortcomings. This belief alone acts as an elixir in good times and bad, enabling you to enjoy and fight the latter.

The Effect on Physical Health

Your emotional health affects your physical health and vice versa. A negative self-image tends to cause chronic stress, headaches, body cramps, and tense muscles. Some people even have digestive problems as a result.

In addition, you are more likely to ignore your health if you do not value yourself. Skipping the gym, missing workouts, being lazy at home, choosing junk and packaged foods over healthy foods, and binge-watching shows when you should be sleeping are some unhealthy practices you are likely to engage in if you do not care much about your well-being.

On the other hand, when you begin to look at yourself from a positive perspective, things begin to improve. You realize that you need to take care of yourself, and you begin to do so. Yes, not everyone with high self-esteem has a good fitness regimen, but at least they realize that fitness is an important element of staying healthy. This realization often leads to an effort to stay fit.

In addition, you are more likely to engage in practices that bring you joy and improve your overall physical and mental well-being. Gradually, you begin to take better care of your health and hygiene and to stay fit and healthy. Engaging in self-care practices slowly becomes a regular part of your life, making you more confident and happier.

Now that you understand the importance of healthy self-esteem, what next? There are things you can do, such as practicing mindfulness, engaging in positive self-talk, adopting a learning mindset, setting boundaries for yourself and others, and having a healthy self-care routine, to boost your self-esteem.

The following chapters discuss these strategies and many more in detail.

But before we get to these strategies, I want to emphasize that increasing your self-esteem can be scary and challenging, especially since there are many myths surrounding the subject. Therefore, I believe it is important that as you begin to improve your self-esteem, you are aware of some of the myths surrounding it so that they do not hold you back and you can move forward with knowledge and understanding.

Chapter 3: The 7 Myths About Self-Esteem

"If self-esteem is a myth, then what is the truth?"

Dr. Christina Hibbert

Like everything else, self-esteem has many myths. If you read the quote above with complete concentration, you will understand that self-esteem is the ultimate truth.

In order for you to have the courage and determination to revive or even rebuild your self-esteem, it is essential that these myths be exploded so that you can fully grasp the concept.

Let's debunk these myths one by one...

Myth #1: Self-esteem and confidence are the same thing

One of the biggest myths in the self-help ecosystem is that self-esteem and confidence are two sides of the same coin. They overlap, but in their true essence they are different.

As we have already established, self-esteem is about whether or not you value and appreciate yourself. It allows you to believe in yourself so that you can unearth your inner potential, refine it, and use it to become the best version of yourself.

Yes, your self-esteem evolves as you go through different life experiences, including the ups and downs of life and interactions with different types of people. Your self-esteem is bound to go through a series of booms and slumps in life, but if you value yourself, you can build your self-esteem even when it takes a big hit.

Conversely, confidence is your ability to believe in yourself and your abilities and talents. I will quote myself on what I said earlier to explain this better.

If you read the beginning of this discussion, you will see the following:

Self-esteem, as we have already established, is about whether or not you value and appreciate yourself. It allows you to believe in yourself so that you can unearth your inner potential, refine it, and use it to become the best version of yourself.

First I reiterated what self-esteem is, and then I mentioned how it gives you the ability to believe in yourself. This ability is what confidence is all about, and it comes from healthy self-esteem.

When your self-esteem is healthy, you believe that you are worth something. This sense of worth gives you the courage to accept that you are great and can do anything if you put your mind to it.

In essence, self-esteem is the foundation of your self-confidence. If you have healthy self-esteem, you are likely to be more confident. You will trust yourself and be willing to discover and improve your hidden talents.

Low self-esteem leads to low self-confidence, which in turn leads to many problems, such as the following

- Poor interpersonal communication skills

- Extreme shyness

- Lack of assertiveness

- Social anxiety

- Bad feelings about yourself

- Inability to realize and follow through on your goals

33

- Avoiding challenging situations, especially when you fear being the focus of everyone's critical judgment

- Expecting the worst outcome from even the most positive situations

- Feeling like a failure.

All of these issues automatically affect your life and everything that goes with it. To feel confident about yourself, you must first strengthen your self-esteem.

Myth #2: Self-esteem comes from the outside

Another common statement associated with self-esteem is that it comes from the outside and not from within, because self-esteem depends on validation and appreciation from those around you, especially the authority figures in your life.

But, is this true? NO, it isn't.

Self-esteem comes only from within. Let's dig deeper into this myth to understand how it comes about.

Our self-esteem begins to develop from the time we are little children. As a child, your well-being, existence, and many life choices depend on others around you, primarily your parents or guardians, and then the adults you usually interact with, such as your aunts, uncles, grandparents, friends of your parents/guardians, school teachers, and so on.

If you grow up in a healthy environment where you receive recognition, love, praise, and respect from your parents and other adults, you will automatically feel good about yourself.

A healthy environment does not necessarily mean no scolding for misbehavior. Yes, your parents may need to scold you, and your teachers will educate you to help you distinguish between right and wrong.

However, if the overall environment is positive, and those around you understand how their words, actions, and behaviors affect little minds, they would be careful in their choice of words and actions to make sure they are teaching you things in a positive way.

On the other hand, if the adults with whom you regularly interact do not understand the consequences of their behavior and how it affects you, they are likely to engage in some practices that could hurt you.

As a child, you may have been told that you were stupid or that you never got the answers right. Maybe there was a lot of yelling in your house. Or maybe you went through some terrible bullying episodes.

People who behave this way have also gone through some hard times in life that have made them who they are. But to get back to the point, such rude and hurtful behavior affects you. You begin to believe that you are inadequate and incapable of doing anything good, or that you are wounded from within.

Our self-perception becomes quite distorted, and we only feel good when someone appreciates us. This feeling is usually temporary and fades after a while.

In one way or another, we become dependent on how others feel about us, which is why many people believe that others define them and that self-esteem comes from the outside.

But the truth is that self-esteem comes from within. It is more like a plant whose seeds are sown and nurtured by us. As we heal and grow, we begin to accurately evaluate ourselves and create our self-image without relying on the opinions and interpretations of others.

Remember, it is your self-esteem; only you can build and nourish it, not those around you. Once you start working on it, you understand that external validation from others is not important. You feel more connected to yourself and can accept yourself as you are and then work on self-development and improvement.

Myth #3: High self-esteem guarantees success

Self-esteem is closely related to the different kinds of success we seek, because how we perceive ourselves affects how we approach different opportunities and challenges in life. This, in turn, influences our choices and whether or not we succeed in the various facets of our lives.

Studies show that those with higher self-esteem tend to be more successful and happier in life, but that's because self-esteem gives you the courage to value yourself.

However, self-esteem is not a guarantee of success. But to understand this better, you must first understand and accept that success is relative. Each of us defines success differently. A popular view is that success is all about making more money. The more money you make and have, the more successful you are.

However, everyone has a different idea of success and a different benchmark. You may think of success as excelling in your career and climbing the corporate ladder, getting promotion after promotion. The more successful you are in your career, the more money you have in your bank account and the more successful you feel.

But that may not be what some of your colleagues think. For others, success may just be about pursuing your passions and being happy with what you do. Perhaps for your sibling, a successful life is one where they have more time for family and are around pure love vibes.

Self-esteem helps you see yourself in a positive light, so you begin to value yourself. It also allows you to evaluate yourself with more objectivity, so you become aware of your shortcomings. Naturally, this helps you improve and make better choices and decisions. As a result, you live a more balanced and holistic life.

Another reason why "self-esteem guarantees success" is a myth is that it tends to put overwhelming pressure on you. It can make you feel that you must excel in every endeavor because you have healthy self-esteem.

This need to excel becomes a toxic perfectionism that makes you strive for perfection in everything. Your self-esteem and confidence take a nosedive when you fail at a project. You feel emotionally crippled and have a hard time getting back up.

You also need to understand that it takes a lot to achieve success and not just healthy self-esteem. For example, you must effectively identify and use opportunities to succeed in life.

You must also be persistent and courageous enough to take risks and experiment to find the best approaches for you. You also need to be super gritty so that you can stick with your goals for the long haul, persevere through tough times, and keep moving toward the finish line.

So yes, self-esteem gives you the stamina to keep going and make your life worthwhile, but it is not the sole criterion for success.

Myth #4: You are born with or without self-esteem

When we see extremely confident people living life on their terms, we often feel that they were born with certain virtues; the same is true with self-esteem.

Many people believe that you are either born with high self-esteem or you are not. This way of thinking may lead you to believe that self-esteem is more of an in-built virtue, and that some people have it from birth, while others don't.

This belief, again, is a great myth. Self-esteem isn't something you're born with; it's a virtue you build as you grow older. It results from the self-perception that forms as you experience life and interact with others and your environment.

Countless people with very low self-esteem work on it, strengthen it, and begin to live a better life. If self-esteem were a built-in virtue, they wouldn't be able to improve it.

The belief that you are born with self-esteem is an ingrained belief that keeps you from growing into a better version of yourself. But you don't want that, do you? In that case, it is best to debunk this myth and know that you can always work on your self-esteem.

Myth #5: Positive affirmations alone can boost self-esteem

Positive affirmations are statements that you practice repeatedly, either by writing them down, saying them out loud, or simply thinking about them, to rewire your brain to think positively. An affirmation is something you believe in completely.

To affirm something, you focus on it or go over that statement or belief again. So if you keep thinking about something, it becomes part of your belief system. Once a thought becomes part of your belief system, it affects your thought process, your attitude, your behavior, your actions, and your life.

Positive affirmations are powerful statements that you should focus on and practice repeatedly to create a more positive mindset. Statements like "I am worthy of good things," "I am confident," "I am happy," and "I am achieving my goals" are excellent examples of positive affirmations that will boost your confidence and, when practiced consistently, rewire your mindset.

So yes, positive affirmations are an extremely beneficial and powerful way to build a positive mindset. As your mindset improves, so does your ability to understand your worth; this establishes that positive affirmations greatly affect your self-esteem.

That's especially true because low self-esteem can be caused by many reasons and issues. For example, positive affirmations won't heal your emotional wounds if you feel inadequate and hurt inside for years. You would need to do more than just chant positive affirmations day in and day out.

You need to identify the root cause of your low self-esteem and then work on different strategies to achieve the desired result: positive self-image.

Also, everyone is different. What works for one person may not work for another. For your friend, positive affirmations may work like a charm, but you may need to equip yourself with more strategies to boost your self-esteem.

In addition, research also shows that positive affirmations work best when there is some reality or evidence to justify them. For example, if you have no accomplishments to your credit and you keep saying, "I am achieving my goals," your brain will have a hard time accepting that. So for positive affirmations to work, you need to structure them based on reality.

It's also important to understand that too many positive affirmations can sometimes make you delusional because you start to feel superior to others; this is not always true, but it's always best to practice everything in moderation.

Positive affirmations are an extremely effective way to boost and strengthen your self-esteem, and you should practice them. An entire chapter of this book is devoted to them. However, relying on them alone may not give your self-esteem the boost it needs.

Myth #6: High self-esteem makes you selfish

With high self-esteem, you begin to understand your true worth. Before, you may have had a low opinion of yourself, but once your self-esteem blossomed, you began to think better of yourself.

Because your self-esteem improves significantly, some people think that this makes them self-centered. Of course, if you become self-centered, you will probably focus more on yourself and less on others, making you a selfish person.

However, this is not true; this does not happen to everyone with high self-esteem. People who truly value themselves and have positive self-esteem understand the pain that those with low self-esteem go through. Out of consideration for their life experiences due to low self-esteem, they try to be compassionate toward those who are struggling. Therefore, self-esteem in its true sense does not make one selfish.

An important point to understand is that it is not selfish to take care of yourself and sometimes say "no" to others. Often, many people who struggle with low self-esteem seek validation from others. This constant need for approval from those around them turns them into people pleasers. Instead of thinking about their needs for a change, they are always rushing to say yes to others, mostly to get approval from those people.

This people-pleasing behavior gives others the upper hand over them, allowing them to take advantage of those with low self-esteem. If you've ever run errands for your bossy brother, or can't say no to your spouse even when you know they're wrong, or are constantly manipulated by your coworker into doing favors for him just so he calls you his friend, you know how it feels.

You forget all about yourself when you get sucked into this vicious cycle of pleasing people. When you work on your self-esteem, you realize how much you have taken yourself for granted over the years. As you begin to value yourself more, you begin to focus on and prioritize your needs. You will pay attention to what feels right for you first, and then do what others ask.

Gradually, the word "no" enters your life, and you find yourself saying no to errands and favors that consume your needs, your peace, and your time. You also begin to make decisions for yourself. No, you are not being mean or selfish, but all those around you who have been abusing you for a long time may see you as selfish.

What you perceive as 'selfishness' is just you taking care of yourself; it is not selfish. It is self-care, and you both deserve and need it. So, no, having high self-esteem does not make you selfish.

Myth #7: Self-esteem is static

Another myth about self-esteem is that it is static. People with this belief think that once you have low self-esteem, there is nothing you can do about it, and that if you have healthy self-esteem, you can never have low self-esteem. Again, this is far from reality.

Your self-esteem is constantly evolving, which means it can improve and it can also decrease. If you have a positive self-esteem, it can go down if you are in a rut. For example, if you lose your job and have no financial means to support yourself, you are likely to feel bad about yourself. This financial burden can cause you to be overly critical of yourself and even question your past life choices.

However, if you equip yourself with the strategies to increase your self-esteem, you can boost it even during this difficult time, giving you the strength to get out of this difficult situation.

You know what self-esteem is now that you have debunked the many popular myths surrounding it. We have cleared up any confusion you may have had about self-esteem. Even if you did not, you will as you continue to read this guide and follow its practical strategies.

Let us move on to the first set of strategies you need to build and improve your self-esteem. You are ready to begin your journey to great self-esteem and personal growth.

NOTE: The journey to building your self-esteem is not a rat race. You are not competing with anyone. Instead, you are just trying to do things to improve yourself. The curve of the journey is different for everyone because we are all unique.

Now that you are reading this book, you have already made a commitment to increase your self-esteem. You need to stick with it and move forward at your own pace. It is okay if that pace is slow. If you read one page of this book, apply even one thing you have learned to your life, and stick with it, you will soon notice the positive effects.

You must continue to take baby steps or big steps, as you choose, and gradually implement the techniques taught in this book. You are amazing and will continue to unlock the brilliant potential you have been hiding for so long. I believe in you and so should you.

Chapter 4: Cultivating Positive Self-Talk

"Change your self-talk. Remind yourself that you are strong and resilient and can handle anything that comes your way."

Anonymous

Positive self-talk is a powerful way to improve your thoughts, feelings, and behavior and empower your self-esteem.

As the quote above says, if you keep reminding yourself how strong and tenacious you are, you can overcome any challenges that come your way. That comes from having the courage to believe in yourself, which comes from how much you value yourself, and what is that?

Yes, self-esteem. It comes down to high self-esteem.

So positive self-talk can help build your self-esteem, but what is positive self-talk? Is there a flip side? What happens when you have positive self-talk? Can you cultivate positive self-talk, and if so, how?

I'm sure these questions are going through your mind right now. They all have answers. There's only one way to find them. Keep moving forward with this book.

What is Self-Talk?

Self-talk is the way we talk to ourselves. Whenever we think about doing something, whether it is deciding what to wear to work, what to cook for dinner, or what career option to pursue, we are having a conversation with ourselves.

This conversation usually takes place quietly inside our heads, but sometimes it can happen out loud. So, for example, when you are thinking about what to cook for dinner, your thoughts and the dialog that goes on in your head is what self-talk is all about.

Let's help you understand this better by continuing with this example.

So, when you are thinking about what to cook, you might have the thought, 'Let's cook spaghetti tonight.' But then, at the same time, you might think, 'I had that last week, so I think

I'll have something else.' And the conversation continues until you decide what to cook.

This example of self-talk is neutral. But it can also have two other tones: positive and negative.

Let's take a look at what they might sound like.

If you have negative self-talk, you might think about how eating spaghetti will affect your fitness routine, which requires you to eat healthy. This thought may make you feel like you can never stick to what you want, which makes you feel bad about yourself. You may end up eating spaghetti, but you may also continue to feel guilty.

If you had positive self-talk, you might skip the spaghetti and replace it with a salad, telling yourself how healthy salads are and how you can stick to your goal of losing a few extra pounds because you are resilient and focused.

Both examples of self-talk affect how you feel and how you behave. In everyday life, we often use self-talk to make different decisions. In addition to affecting our decisions, self-talk also affects our moods.

Let's continue with another example. Suppose you decide to apply for your dream job. In this case, you're likely to have some fears and doubts about whether or not you'll get it, and if you do get it, whether or not you'll be able to do it successfully, or perhaps whether or not you have what it takes to apply for it in the first place.

These insecurities and concerns are natural. However, if you have positive self-talk, you will tell yourself that it is okay to have such doubts, but that you have the skills and accomplishments to get the job.

If you don't yet have an impressive resume to get the job, you will gently tell yourself to work on meeting the requirements and apply next year. In either case, you are likely to do the right thing for yourself and feel good about yourself.

On the other hand, if you had negative self-talk, you would talk yourself out of applying for the job by constantly shifting your focus to your lack of accomplishments and inability to get the job. Even if you somehow convince yourself to apply for the job, you are likely to be certain that you won't get it and may even regret applying.

Even reading this account may seem a bit stressful, right? Imagine how hard it must be for those who constantly engage in negative self-talk.

Next, we will explore the consequences of negative self-talk.

How Negative Self-Talk Undermines Your Self-Esteem

Being critical of yourself or telling yourself not to do something is not a bad thing. If you think about something dangerous and talk yourself out of it, that is good, right? Similarly, if you evaluate yourself and point out your weaknesses, that is not a bad thing.

However, if you constantly ridicule yourself and point out your shortcomings to prove your incompetence, that is unhealthy. This behavior creates an inner critic that is always ready to spit venom at you when you feel like pursuing your passions, experimenting with something, or trying to do something that brings you joy.

This voice has a pessimistic tone and makes you focus only on negative outcomes and your mistakes. Statements like "I'm incapable of achieving my goals," "I'll never learn to cook well," or "I'm sure I won't get promoted this year because I suck at my job" are examples of your inner critic. With such an inner critic, you have a very negative monologue.

Suppose you were considering applying to an Ivy League university earlier. In this case, you can weigh the pros and cons and the chances of getting into your desired school. However, if you have chronic negative self-talk, you are likely to focus only on how you will never get into an Ivy League school because you are incompetent. Your inner critic will probably stop at nothing to point out your ineptitude.

So, having an inner critic has a strong and harsh effect on your self-esteem. It makes you feel worthless, which lowers your self-esteem. It makes you filter out all the positive and think only about the negative. Most of the time, negative self-talk is repetitive. It keeps projecting your failures, insecurities, fears, and struggles onto yourself to confirm your inadequacy.

The more you think along the negative lines, the lower your self-esteem drops. As your self-esteem takes a big hit, so does your confidence. Gradually, you stop believing in yourself, which affects your ability to stay strong and courageously face adversity.

You begin to run away from your problems so that you don't have to face them. You are also likely to give up easily and not take risks. These behavioral changes affect every aspect of your life.

You find it hard to concentrate or to strive for improvement. In addition, you stop doing things that bring you joy, mainly because the sadness of all your failures engulfs you.

Your stress also affects your relationships, making you either too grumpy to be cordial with anyone, or too sad to focus on anyone but your problems. Either way, it affects your relationships. That's how powerful and damaging negative self-talk is.

But you know what? There is a bright side. There is positive self-talk, and it is the elixir to beat negative self-talk and boost your self-esteem.

Let's learn more about it.

The Transformative Power of Positive Self-Talk

You have the power to change the way you think and feel. Optimism is a choice you can easily make. It allows you to ignore the negatives associated with a situation and focus on the positives.

By accomplishing this feat, you equip yourself with the power to let go of your problems, acknowledge your blessings, find solutions, and be happy with what you have.

There are several ways to accomplish this, and one of the most effective approaches is to cultivate positive self-talk.

Positive self-talk gives you the belief that you have wings to fly and the courage to find them. The more you practice it, the more persistent you become. Once you find your wings, you soon realize that you can spread them. When you spread them, you get the courage to flap them and take flight. Soon you begin to fly and then soar high in the sky. The feeling of being free, powerful and brilliant is amazing.

But how does positive self-talk bring about such changes?

It changes the tone of your self-talk from positive to negative: The first step in changing your negative mindset to a positive one is to feed yourself some positive thoughts. A mindset is a set of beliefs that affect how you perceive everything around you. It affects your thoughts, feelings, emotions, attitudes, and behaviors.

If you have a long history of negative self-talk, your mindset is likely to be negative. Constantly repeating debilitating thoughts and focusing on the negative changes your perception and ability to think clearly. However, when you begin to feed yourself positive thoughts, you gradually change the tone of your self-talk.

Suggestions such as "I'm a good person," "I can achieve my goals," "If I try, I can be good at accounting," "It's okay if I failed, I'll try harder next time," gradually change the tone of your self-talk from extremely harsh to calmer and kinder.

This gradually encourages your mind to think positively: As the tone of your self-talk improves, so does your mind's ability to think better.

If you used to think of yourself as a "lost cause" every time you made a mistake or succumbed to a challenge, you can now calm yourself down and think optimistically instead. Instead of feeling that your life is a mess, you will tell yourself that life can be difficult sometimes, but you can make things easier and smoother.

It helps build positive beliefs and turns pessimistic views into optimistic ones: The ability to think positively helps you build positive beliefs that shape how you think, act, and behave.

Belief is the acceptance of something as true. For example, if you are sure that your friend "Janet" is being honest with you, that is your belief. Similarly, we have beliefs about the world around us and about ourselves.

Your beliefs play a monumental role in shaping your decisions. If you believe you cannot get a certain job, you will probably not apply. If you believe you will not be successful in running your business, you are likely to give up when you encounter a setback.

However, if you begin to think positively through positive self-talk, you will slowly change your negative beliefs to positive beliefs and create more optimistic and healthier beliefs.

For example, if you have tried and failed to learn how to drive a car, you are likely to believe that you can never learn to drive. But if you start having positive self-talk, you slowly begin to believe that if you put your mind to it, you can learn to drive. Over time, positive self-talk rewires your mind to think positively, so you cultivate many healthy beliefs that positively shape your life.

It gives you the courage to believe in yourself: Self-belief can be quite challenging if you keep putting yourself down with negative self-talk. If you hear negative things about yourself day after day, you are likely to believe that you are incompetent.

On the other hand, when you begin to talk to yourself in a positive way, you begin to realize that you are not half as bad as you think. With time and consistency, you begin to accept and like yourself and build the courage to believe in yourself.

It helps you to find out your abilities: As you begin to believe in yourself, you find it easier to explore and unlock your potential. You now know that you are good enough, and you begin to find out what you are good at. Once you figure that out, you can improve your potential and become a better version of yourself.

It helps you understand that no weakness is permanent: We all have weaknesses and shortcomings, and having them is perfectly natural and normal. Unfortunately, when you have negative self-talk, you also build a fixed mindset.

There are two basic types of mindsets: fixed and growth. Those with a fixed mindset believe that they are born with a certain level of potential that cannot be improved. They also believe that shortcomings are permanent because they cannot improve them.

In contrast, people with a growth mindset believe that they can always improve and become a better version of themselves. Nothing is permanent, not even shortcomings, and if you try, you can excel at anything you want.

When you practice positive self-talk on a regular basis, you cultivate a growth mindset. Cultivating a growth mindset helps you understand that it is perfectly human to have weaknesses and even negative virtues. However, you can improve on them and overcome the hurdles you face in your self-development.

It nudges you toward the path of self-improvement: When you begin to accept your weaknesses and the fact that they are not permanent, you begin to work on improving yourself. Instead of constantly criticizing yourself for your shortcomings, you accept them and lovingly work on them.

This motivates you to face and overcome challenges: As you become a more refined version of yourself, you also build the stamina and strength to face life's hardships. Not only do you face them courageously, but you also find ways to combat and resolve them.

If you used to think about quitting your job every time your boss gave you a hard time, you now look for ways to be better at your job so that you no longer give your boss opportunities to lose his temper with you. Similarly, you become more resilient and begin to feel optimistic about life.

These changes make you more confident and positive, and give you the courage to face life's ups and downs with greater strength. As a result, your self-esteem rises to a whole new level and you can do whatever your heart desires.

How do you cultivate this magical ability to speak positively to yourself? Don't worry, we have the solution for you. Let's get to it.

How to Cultivate Positive Self-Talk

Your mind is indeed extremely powerful and beautiful. You just need to train it to work in the right direction. Once you do that, you become invincible. Yes, even the sky will no longer be your limit.

Let me teach you how to equip yourself with one of the basic tools to accomplish this - self-talk.

Observe Your Self-Talk

The path to changing a behavior begins with observation. You must observe and understand the problem at hand before you can begin to work on it. The same goes for cultivating positive self-talk.

Therefore, observing your self-talk is the first step to improving your self-talk. Here's how to do it:

Take a 5-minute break from whatever you are doing and tune in to your thoughts.

Gently observe the nature of the thoughts that are circulating in your mind right now. Pick a few and write them down. For example, if you are working on your office project or college assignment and you are unable to complete it, write down this thought: "I cannot work on this project/assignment.

Take a deep breath, inhaling through your nose and exhaling gently through your mouth. Take another deep cleansing breath. Now take a third. Deep breathing promotes relaxation in your body, relaxes your mind, and makes it easier to think clearly without becoming anxious.

Next, observe the thought you have written down. If you can't write it down or don't feel like it, that's okay. Just focus on the thought in your mind.

How do you feel when you think about this thought? Does it upset you? Do you feel anxious? Do you feel incompetent? Write down how you feel or say the feeling out loud. You can even record yourself saying it to observe it again later.

Once you have written down your observations, take another deep breath and calm yourself.

Now that you have observed what negative thoughts look and feel like, you need to look for such statements in your self-talk.

You need to take frequent "observation" breaks throughout the day. The more you observe your self-talk, the more you'll get the hang of what your self-talk looks like.

Accept that you have negative self-talk

The next step is to accept that you have negative self-talk. Acceptance is the second fundamental step in working on your problem. Once you accept a particular problem, you can work on resolving it.

Often we know we have a problem, but we keep denying it, and this unspoken denial only makes the problem worse because it keeps us from working on the root cause.

In this case, once you have observed and realized that you are practicing negative self-talk, you need to accept it; this will solidify your acceptance and encourage you to address it.

Now say out loud, "I have negative self-talk and I am committed to working on it. Say it slowly, clearly and loudly about five times, then write it down.

So far you have been calm and positive. You may not realize the effect of this acceptance right now, but it has signaled your brain to work very gently on the problem at hand, 'negative self-talk.

Set the intention to build positive self-talk

Once you have accepted that you are practicing negative self-talk, you need to set the intention to change it to positive self-talk.

Setting the intention shows your commitment to the issue and to working to improve it. When you set the intention, you focus on the issue and begin to take it seriously.

To set the intention to create positive self-talk, think about how your negative self-talk has held you back over the years.

Make sure you focus on the detrimental effect and how it has kept you from doing everything you have wanted to do for a long time. The adventure trips you missed, the scholarships you never applied for, the promotions you never tried for, that crush you really liked but never had the courage to talk to, and all the things you could not do because your inner critic kept telling you not to.

Hold that pain, take a deep breath, and channel it positively. Now write down the intention to cultivate positive self-talk. You could write something like, "I am committed to building positive self-talk and I am actively working on it," "I set the intention to cultivate positive self-talk to increase my self-esteem," or something along those lines.

As you write down your intention, remember to use only positive words.

Once you have written it down, repeat it out loud. Say it a few times. You are likely to feel positive about yourself; this is the power of positive intentions and self-talk - it makes you optimistic.

Don't just write and read your intention once; read it every day, at least twice. Please set an alarm to read your intention and practice it once in the morning before you start your routine chores and then again before you go to bed. The former sets a positive tone for the day by reminding you of your intention to speak positively to yourself, and the latter tells your brain to think about it while you sleep.

Research shows that your brain is active even when you are asleep. If you want to focus on something, reminding yourself of it before you go to sleep activates your brain to actively think about it. So, repeating your intention before you go to sleep makes your brain actively work to accept it and make it your belief.

Add 'Yet' to Your Self-Talk

'Yet' is a subtle but very powerful word. It can change the course of your self-talk very gently and significantly. Carol Dweck, one of the pioneers of mindset research, suggests that adding yet to your language helps reframe the tone of your self-talk.

Let's illustrate this with an example:

Imagine for a moment that you are learning how to swim. If you do not get the hang of it on your fourth attempt, you will probably say something like, "I cannot swim" or "I can never learn to swim. Now, both of these statements have a negative connotation. They suggest that you cannot swim or that you will never learn to swim. These classic examples of fixed mindsets remind you of your inability to learn a skill.

Now let us reframe them with the word 'yet'. Adding 'yet' to these two statements changes them to: 'I cannot yet swim' and 'I have not yet learned to swim. While these statements still state that you cannot swim and that you cannot learn to swim, they also give you hope that you cannot swim now, but there is a chance that you can learn to swim in the future.

The 'yet' adds hope to otherwise negative and gloomy statements. It encourages you to believe in yourself and in your ability to accomplish a task or work toward a goal.

So, every time you find yourself saying something you cannot do, add "yet" to it and it will instantly brim with hope and positivity.

Harness the Power of Positive Affirmations

As mentioned earlier in this guide, positive affirmations are positive statements that you believe to be true: anything you affirm to yourself is something you accept as the truth.

Over the years, you have mostly affirmed negative thoughts to yourself. Things like "I'm terrible," "I lost my chance to grow," "I'm not worthy of love," "I don't deserve success and respect," and the like have been drilled into your head.

All of these negative statements were part of your system. In a way, you have been affirming them to yourself. These negative affirmations have affected your attitudes, behaviors and decisions.

To counteract their effect, you need to harness the power of positive affirmations. Positive affirmations are simple statements that you affirm to yourself by focusing on them, repeating them verbally, or writing them down.

As you repeat such suggestions to yourself, your mind begins to accept them and then gradually incorporates them into your belief system. As your belief system improves, your self-esteem begins to change for the better. Brilliant, right?

Now let's look at how you can practice positive affirmations:

Decide whether you want to practice positive affirmations by writing them down or recording/speaking them; this will help you prepare the affirmations accordingly. If you want to write them down, keep a journal and pen/pencil/marker nearby so you don't have to search for these items when you begin your affirmation session. If you just want to speak, keep a tape recorder handy or open a voice recorder on your phone.

Next, sit somewhere quiet and peaceful. You can sit in a noisy environment, but when you begin affirmations (or any practice that requires your utmost concentration), you need to be fully focused in order to get the most out of it. Being in a noisy place will distract you, so it is best to do it in a quiet place.

When you are ready, take a few deep breaths to calm yourself.

Next, think about the virtue you want to instill in yourself, a goal you want to achieve, or an improvement you want to make. For example, if you want to work harder to graduate with flying colors, that might be the goal you want to affirm to yourself.

If you want to feel happier from within, you can create an affirmation about that. Since we are specifically talking about increasing our self-esteem, let's take that as our goal and create a positive affirmation.

Now you need to write down or think of a statement that focuses on this goal. It should be concise, positive and present oriented.

It should be short because long affirmations are harder to practice and remember. Instead of writing, "I want to improve my self-esteem because I have been sad and feel inadequate for love and respect, and I want to make more friends," you can say, "I am working on improving my self-esteem so that I can live a more fulfilling life.

It should be positive because the subconscious mind pays more attention to positive words and leaves out words with negative connotations. Instead of saying, 'I am not going to put myself down,' you can say, 'I am going to talk nice to myself. Your subconscious mind removes words such as "not," "won't," "can't," and the like, which changes the statement into something different from what you had planned. In this case, the affirmation becomes, 'I will degrade myself. That's not what you want, is it?

Finally, the affirmation must be present-oriented so that your mind is focused on actualizing it in the present moment, not in the future. Often, when we want a certain change, we focus on the future. For example, you might say, "I will become happier," "I want to improve my self-esteem," or "My self-esteem will improve. While these statements are concise and positive, they are future-centered, meaning that the change you want will happen in the next few days.

On the other hand, you want the result in the present, but you don't know why you can't manifest it. It's primarily because your subconscious mind is focused on creating that change in the future.

However, suppose you change your affirmation to "I am happy," "I am actively working on improving my self-esteem and it is increasing," or "My self-esteem is high. In this case, you will begin to see positive results in the present moment.

Your mind becomes active and makes you engage in activities that help you materialize your goal in the here and now, not in the near future. As a result, you manifest what you want. Therefore, when you create a positive affirmation, center it in the present.

In this particular case, some positive affirmations you can use are "I am brimming with self-esteem," "My self-esteem is constantly improving," "I feel good about myself," "I appreciate and love myself," "I have high self-esteem," "I accept and appreciate myself," "I value myself," "I have positive self-esteem and spread positivity around," "I am actively working on raising my self-esteem," and "I am a channel of positivity.

Now you need to slowly and confidently say this affirmation out loud about ten times. Make sure your voice is loud enough to be heard and focused. Speak each word clearly and slowly so that its vibration rings in your ears and strengthens your focus.

Try to get as emotionally involved with the affirmation as possible when you are practicing it verbally so that you begin to believe the suggestion. Belief is an incredibly powerful emotion; you perceive something as truth when you put your belief into it. This truth influences your belief system and causes you to harness the power of the universe and attract positive experiences.

Once you have finished saying the affirmation, please write it down at least ten times. It is better to repeat the affirmation aloud as you write it.

After completing the steps, tune in and examine your feelings. You will probably feel much more positive and lighter than before. Write down your feelings in a journal or record them as you speak to keep track of them.

Take short 5-minute positive affirmation breaks throughout the day. Practice positive affirmations after working on a task for 2 to 3 hours or when you are feeling emotionally low. In addition, create more positive affirmations that focus on improvements you want to make in yourself.

Here are the affirmations you can practice:

I am happy and radiate happiness.

I feel peaceful and calm inside.

I am confident in my abilities.

I explore and develop my potential.

I spend quality time with myself and feel good about it.

I breathe in peace and breathe out stress.

I radiate positive vibes wherever I go.

I feel confident that I can achieve my goals.

I value and appreciate myself.

I am satisfied with my life and work hard to improve it.

I feel blessed with all that I have in life.

I believe in my ability to do well in life.

I set and achieve achievable goals.

I am in full control of my life.

I take constructive feedback in a positive way and use it where needed.

I am confident and face challenges with courage.

Feel free to add other positive affirmations to this list. If you follow the guidelines above, you are good to go!

Practice Creative Visualization

Creative visualization involves using imagery to train your mind to think creatively and positively in order to achieve a specific goal. It is not a strategy that will directly improve your self-talk. However, it is a powerful tool for improving self-esteem, practicing positive affirmations, and affirming optimistic ideas.

We have already mentioned how we affirm things by focusing on them. When you constantly focus on something, your brain begins to think in that direction. For example, you feel confident when you visualize yourself doing well in life, feeling more confident, living a happy life, thriving in your career, and having great relationships. You are confident that you can achieve all these goals.

You mentally rehearse for success by fostering a sense of adequacy and strengthening your belief in your ability to achieve all your goals. Instead of being ruled by negative thoughts, you become the ultimate driver of your mindset. You are given the power and ability to shape your thoughts and beliefs. As a result, your self-esteem soars and you move toward the life you desire.

Let us look at an example to help you understand this more deeply. Take a deep breath and imagine yourself feeling relaxed and light. Now imagine that you are lying on a beautiful beach, looking at the scenery and enjoying the sun. Stay with this image for two minutes. You feel calmer than before, don't you? That's the transformative power of creative visualization.

Now let us look at how to practice creative visualization.

Sit comfortably in whatever way you like. If you prefer to stand, do so.

Take a few deep, calming breaths to re-center yourself.

When you feel a little more focused, close your eyes.

Think about how you feel about yourself and how you value yourself. It is okay if the self-review is not so positive.

Now think about how you want to see yourself and how much you want to value yourself.

Make a mental picture of it. For example, think about how you would feel if you felt more confident and greater about yourself. Perhaps making more money or becoming the head of your department would increase your self-esteem. Imagine yourself in that position.

As you do this, say about five times, "My self-esteem is high and I feel great about myself.

Do this for a total of three to five minutes. You can do it longer, but five minutes is a good start.

Let's not overwhelm ourselves and build good habits by taking small steps.

Now open your eyes and write or talk about how you feel - if you choose to talk about it, record yourself. Chances are you will feel energized with newfound motivation and improved self-esteem.

You can create mental images of different goals you want to achieve. For example, you can think about feeling happy, starting your art project, being around loved ones, eating healthy and becoming more physically fit, thinking about how appreciated you feel in general, etc.

You are free to think of anything and everything that will improve your self-esteem each day.

It is best to do this exercise for 5 minutes every day. Even better is to do it twice a day. Also, whenever you feel hurt or have low self-esteem, close your eyes and visualize yourself doing well and overcoming the problems in your life. Just 2 to 5 minutes of creative visualization can improve your mood and self-esteem.

Create a Gratitude Journal

Your blessings shape your attitude and your life. When you are grateful for something, you immediately feel happy and hopeful because you know there is light at the end of the tunnel.

In contrast, when you ignore your blessings, you focus more on your problems: no money, no honest friends to talk to, not even one good suit to wear, no time to pursue your passion projects, not enough money to do what your heart desires, and so on. The list goes on.

Of course, when you pay more attention to your problems than your blessings, your mindset becomes negative because you feed it all the wrong things, which can lead to chronic stress. This focus affects your self-talk and your ability to think clearly during difficult times. Therefore, gratitude is critical to creating positive self-talk.

Gratitude shifts your focus from what you don't have and all the things that may not be going your way to all that you do have. When you start thinking about gratitude, even having a glass of water to drink feels like a HUGE blessing. This is the beautiful power of gratitude.

So here is how you can practice gratitude to encourage positive self-talk:

When you wake up each day, think of one thing you are grateful for. It could be the ability to walk, to wake up another day, to sleep peacefully, to have a comfortable bed, or anything else. If possible, write it down in your journal. It is best to devote a section of your journal to counting your blessings.

You can also keep a separate gratitude journal, but often this becomes too much work for people, so I advise them to have a "gratitude" section in their regular journal. If writing is not your thing, make a small recording of what you are grateful for.

When you take a shower, be grateful for that. When you eat breakfast, say how blessed you feel.

Continue to count your blessings throughout the day.

Count any five things you were especially thankful for during the day. It could be anything from how your boss appreciated your work, to how nice your neighbor was to pick up your mail while you were out, to a good lunch with your friend, to just coming home and feeling relaxed. Write down or record these blessings.

Set reminders and alarms to write down your blessings. The first two to three weeks will be tough because it is hard to build a new habit, but you can do it! After three weeks, you'll get the hang of this practice. After a month, you'll notice small blessings all around you.

Be sure to review your gratitude list once a week. These blessings will pull you back whenever you feel sad and restore your positivity.

Reframe Challenges and Embrace Them

Our self-talk shapes our perception and vice versa. Most of the time, negative self-talk happens when we're facing a challenge. For example, maybe you have a big deadline to meet and you start questioning your ability and thinking you won't be able to meet it, or maybe you have a big fight with your partner and you immediately think they might leave you.

To become optimistic and increase your self-esteem, you need to develop the ability to reframe challenges and embrace them instead of letting them scare you. When you reframe challenges, you see them as routine, manageable instances and/or opportunities for growth.

Instead of being intimidated by a huge deadline looming over your head, start planning to work on the project and begin building momentum. Instead of thinking that your partner is going to leave you, think of ways to find a middle ground, try to understand your partner's perspective, and then explain yours to improve the situation.

When facing a difficult or even mildly stressful situation, take a deep breath. Breathe in through your nose to a count of 4 and out through your mouth to a longer count, say 5 or 6.

Deep breathing relaxes your stressed nerves and creates the mental space for clearer thinking. So when you take a few deep breaths, you find it easy to reframe your debilitating thoughts into uplifting ones.

Now think about the challenges and thoughts that are upsetting you.

If possible, write them down.

Next, gently tweak the negative thoughts by removing negative words from the statements and replacing them with positive substitutes.

For example, if you used to think, "I won't be able to meet the deadline," change the "won't" to "will" and say, "I will be able to meet the deadline" or "I will start working on the project so that I can meet the deadline successfully.

Once your statement sounds positive enough, affirm it to yourself by repeating it a few times and writing it with deep conviction.

When you feel a little more motivated, start working on the challenge.

Also, tell yourself that the challenge is not a problem, but an opportunity to improve. Continuing with the example of a big deadline, think of it as a chance to prove yourself.

Make this a routine practice and you will begin to find yourself better able to deal with the various setbacks in your life.

Celebrate small victories

Positive self-talk comes from kindness and appreciation.

When you face a challenge, be kind to yourself. Similarly, you need to appreciate yourself when you achieve something, no matter how small.

Because of our old negative self-talk habits, we're often too hard on ourselves, even when it's not warranted. For example, you may have landed a job after several unsuccessful interviews, but instead of celebrating this small accomplishment, you remind yourself of your incompetence.

Of course, when you resort to putting yourself down, your inner critic gets stronger and your negative self-talk becomes all the more monstrous. On the contrary, when you acknowledge your small victories, you find the inner courage to see your potential. You feel a little more confident, and instead of criticizing yourself, you encourage yourself to move forward.

This encouragement is what you need to face your problems and overcome them. As a result, your self-esteem blossoms.

So, how do you learn to celebrate your small victories?

Pay attention to how you work and what you work on in your daily routine. If you are going to send 100 emails to existing clients, make a note of it. If you are going to walk 1000 steps today as part of your new fitness program, pay attention to that.

After you send 100 emails or take 1000 steps, acknowledge it.

Whether you cooked today's lunch, came back to work after a week's absence, spoke positively to yourself, or did something that had a positive impact on you, pat yourself on the back for it.

Also, say nice things to yourself like, "Good job: I did it!' 'Oh wow, I did that right,' 'I'm proud of myself,' and similar positive things to boost your morale.

Also, make a conscious effort to write down these small victories so that each time you read these reports, you will be reminded of all the good things you continue to do.

You may not notice the positive effect of this strategy right now, but in a few days you will find yourself thinking more positively than before. You'll also notice a significant decrease in your constant self-battering.

Now that you have gone through the various techniques you can use to cultivate positive self-talk to boost your self-esteem, try to create a routine of these practices by stacking them. This approach helps each habit become a trigger for the other. For example, if you practice affirmations in the morning and then write down your blessings, your affirmations will remind you to do the next practice.

As your self-talk improves, so does your ability to think for yourself. Low self-esteem makes us vulnerable to behaviors that directly or indirectly cause us to neglect our own needs. However, when you begin to talk to yourself gently and kindly, you begin to value yourself. This, in turn, makes you focus on yourself and practice some self-love. Well, that's what we're going to talk about next.

Let's go to the next chapter and talk about the role of self-love in increasing your self-esteem and how to practice it.

Chapter 5: Practicing Self-Love

"No other love, no matter how genuine it is, can fulfill one's heart better than unconditional self-love."

Edmond Mbiaka

Here is the truth...We keep seeking love, validation, and respect from others without realizing that no matter how much love and validation you get from people, that will not satisfy you until you learn to love yourself.

You may have come across the "empty cup" analogy, which suggests that if you can't pour from an empty cup, you can't give love, respect, and care to others unless you have the same for yourself.

So what is self-love? How is it critical to building healthy self-esteem? How can you practice it? Let's find answers to these questions.

Self-love - Beyond self-indulgence

Self-love, as the name suggests, is about loving yourself without judgment and in a way that fully accepts you.

Self-acceptance is a fundamental part of self-love. It is about accepting yourself wholeheartedly and unconditionally. Whether you are tall or short, skinny or overweight, stammer when you speak or stutter when you sing, walk differently than everyone else, have a funny walk, procrastinate or be proactive, you simply accept who you are.

Once you start accepting yourself with all your flaws, weaknesses, shortcomings, strengths, qualities, and habits, you can easily feel comfortable in your skin and gradually start to like and love yourself more.

Some argue that self-love is about self-indulgence and will make you a mean, self-centered and spoiled person. This is not true!

Self-love is recognizing and appreciating who you are, which fosters spiritual, psychological, physical, and emotional growth. It is an ongoing process that teaches you several things about yourself, including the following

- Who you are as a person

- Your interests, likes, and dislikes

- Your passions and ambitions

- What works for you and what doesn't

- How to set boundaries for yourself and others to achieve mental peace

- Your needs, wants and desires

- How to best take care of yourself

- When, why, and how to forgive yourself so you can move on

- Accepting your imperfections while recognizing your inherent worth.

Many of us have a habit of being overly critical of ourselves. You may not be happy with your smoking habit, but instead of finding ways to quit, you continue to put yourself down and continue to smoke. You may not be too proud of your procrastination, but you focus more on criticizing yourself and less on overcoming this unhealthy habit.

However, this changes for the better when healthy self-love is in place. Instead of constantly beating yourself up for one mistake after another, you accept that having faults and making mistakes is human.

It is important to understand that self-acceptance does not make you self-obsessed. Instead, it encourages you to accept your shortcomings and gradually work to overcome them because you begin to value yourself. So yes, self-love has a powerful and positive effect on your self-esteem.

Let's take a look at why self-love is crucial for healthy self-esteem.

Why Self-love is Essential for Healthy Self-Esteem

Self-love is essential to your well-being and does wonders for your self-esteem. This happens for several reasons.

It lowers your stress level: We often feel stressed because we feel unable to face and handle the challenges we face. When you love yourself, you begin to appreciate yourself. You can even handle the self-critical thoughts that add to your stress. As a result, your stress level decreases.

In addition, self-love makes you put yourself first whenever and wherever necessary. You start making time for yourself and doing things that bring you joy, which reduces your stress and increases your self-esteem.

It makes you more resilient: Stress, negative thoughts, and low self-belief can make you give in to challenges too easily. You avoid facing your problems because you are sure you cannot handle them.

However, when you begin to love yourself, you are kinder and more patient with yourself. Instead of surrendering to problems, you accept how you feel, calm down, and determine the root cause of your behavior.

It may take some time to face and deal with your problems, but eventually you will. An increased sense of resilience boosts your self-esteem and makes you more likely to face challenges head-on.

It encourages you to take risks: Stepping out of your comfort zone isn't easy. Trying new things, especially taking big risks, is a no-no for many of us. But some of us can take risks and experiment. This happens best when we believe in ourselves, know that we can handle the outcome, and that it is okay to try different things whether we like the overall experience or not.

When you begin to accept and love yourself, you begin to nurture the belief that you are worth any investment in yourself and that you can take any risk you want. You begin to take chances, and as you move outside your comfort zone, you begin to think outside the box. This ability to think and live freely also gives your self-esteem a massive boost.

You can better identify growth opportunities: Lack of self-belief makes us unaware of many growth opportunities. If you constantly feel that you cannot achieve your goals, make it big in your field, or overcome a challenge, it is natural to become oblivious to the various opportunities that lie ahead. Since you know you cannot make the most of them, why even try?

With self-love in the picture, things begin to change for the better. As you take care of yourself, you begin to spend time with yourself, which gives you insight into your potential. Instead of dismissing your abilities, you begin to explore and sharpen them, which helps you identify opportunities and use them well.

You may not take advantage of every opportunity, but some are likely to turn out very well for you. Such successes build your confidence and self-esteem.

Do what you love: Our lives are full of responsibilities, such as work, children, family, friends, household chores, and so on. With so much to do, we rarely have time for ourselves. It is time to do things we love, things that calm us down, activities that excite us, those that make us smile, and those that bring out the inner crazy in us.

Now, it's not about not having enough time, it's more about getting our priorities right. We don't make time for ourselves because we rarely prioritize ourselves. This attitude takes a positive turn when we have self-love.

We still fulfill our obligations, but we begin to focus on ourselves and make time for things that bring us peace, happiness, excitement, thrill, love, and prosperity. When you start doing things you love, you start to like yourself more, and your self-esteem increases.

Pour out love: Going back to the empty cup analogy, if you don't have love for yourself, you can pour love out to others, but it's not pure. You may have noticed how difficult it is to smile in front of your loved ones when you are feeling upset and frustrated from within.

You spend time with them without fully participating in the experience. You may also find that you easily lose your temper and your composure. On the other hand, when you cultivate self-love, the void within begins to fill in. You know that you are here for yourself, no matter what. This belief alone is enough to calm you down in stressful situations.

And when you begin to overflow with sincere and pure love for yourself, it becomes easier to project it outward. You begin to spend quality time with others, listen better to your loved ones, pay attention to their needs, and show affection. As a result, your relationships improve, and when you see yourself surrounded by true and loving relationships, your self-esteem improves.

Set healthy boundaries with yourself and others: Unfortunately, low self-esteem and a lack of self-love almost always lead you to seek validation from others. When you depend on the approval of others, you begin to give them too much right over yourself. Their word becomes your final command. You let others decide what you need to do in life.

Saying "no" to others becomes too difficult for you, and slowly you begin to lose your voice, which has a detrimental effect on your sense of self-worth. I understand how traumatizing this feeling can be, but the good news is that self-love actually improves it. Giving yourself unconditional love allows you to understand how important you are and that you are the ultimate director of yourself.

Taking suggestions from others and agreeing with what they say is fine if it is what you want and what works for you. But you stop letting them control you. You begin to think for yourself instead of bowing to what others say.

As a result, you begin to analyze your relationships and how they affect you, and you begin to set healthy boundaries for yourself and especially for them.

Instead of letting people boss you around, you communicate your needs and concerns to them and begin to build meaningful and healthy relationships. You value yourself even more as you see yourself triumphing in this area.

It helps you find your purpose in life: Many of us don't know our true purpose, which explains why we feel lost. We have a lot to do, but we don't feel very happy when we think about where our lives are going. This problem is rooted in many factors, including a lack of self-awareness and self-love.

Self-acceptance and self-love allow you to spend quality time with yourself. As you understand yourself more and more, you begin to figure out your purpose or calling. Loving yourself also makes you spiritual. Spirituality is a very relative term that is defined differently by different people.

But the essence of it is to find the right direction for yourself. You steer in that direction when you know what you are meant to do. You begin to invest time in meaningful activities, engage in positive interactions with the right people, and focus on what truly aligns with your life's purpose. Your happiness levels also increase manifold, and the quality of your life improves.

Let us now discuss some common obstacles to practicing self-love and how to effectively overcome them so that you can learn to love yourself wholeheartedly.

How to Overcome the Obstacles to Self-love

Every journey we begin and every goal we pursue has obstacles; the same principle applies to self-love.

Self-love should come naturally to us; however, challenges shroud this journey. Regardless of our sincerest intentions to love ourselves, it can be a bit of an uphill task to shake off old mindsets, beliefs, and habits that we have practiced and normalized for so long.

Because we are all different, unique individuals, we are likely to experience different obstacles. You will experience certain common issues on your journey to love yourself.

Let us review them one by one so that you can easily recognize them when they arise and how best to deal with them.

Obstacle #1: The Comparison Game

Comparison is a great way to decide which Android phone to buy, which business to invest in, which brand of pasta to buy, which coach to consult, which book to read over the weekend, and so on. But comparison is not a healthy path to take when it comes to ourselves and others.

Throughout the day we have various virtual and physical interactions with others, often a combination of both. Every time we see or meet someone who looks great, has a successful career, lives a luxurious life, or does things we want to do, we experience a sense of longing.

Similarly, when we scroll through our social media feeds, we see posts, stories, and status updates of people taking exquisite vacations, closing huge business deals, and doing noble, fun, and exciting things we only dream about.

This yearning is usually accompanied by personal dissatisfaction, insecurity, doubt, and inadequacy. When such feelings arise, we tend to compare ourselves too much with others. This comparison usually produces a long list of our shortcomings and incompetence.

Occasional self-comparison, where you draw inspiration from others without belittling yourself, isn't unhealthy. But if you constantly criticize yourself for not being as good as someone else, you have a problem. This makes you feel bad about yourself and can lower your self-confidence, satisfaction, and self-actualization.

So, comparison is a pretty big obstacle that can get in the way of your self-love and self-esteem journey. So how do we solve it?

List and acknowledge your strengths: Just as you learned to list your blessings in the previous chapter, you need to list all your qualities and good points. Set an alarm titled "List My Strengths" for any time of the day when you have a little free time. Just 5 minutes is enough.

When the alarm goes off, close everything and take a short "self-acknowledgment" break. Write down everything you like about yourself. From your hair, to your eyes, to the way you speak, to your honesty, to your drive to be better, to helping strangers, to just showing up for work - it can be anything.

The goal is to come up with at least one thing you like about yourself. Once you have listed this quality, think about how happy it makes you feel and how much you appreciate yourself. You can say things like, "I am happy that I have great hair" or "I appreciate my ability to stay honest even in difficult situations. Feel free to add more qualities to the list at any time.

Build on the list and read it daily: Review your list of strengths, especially before you start your routine tasks and whenever you see someone doing better.

The list will be short at first, but within a week it will have about six or more things you like about yourself. That's when the real party starts. Soon you will feel more confident and find it easier to resist the urge to compare yourself to others.

Remember the list: When you find yourself comparing yourself to others and looking for flaws, remember this "list of strengths. Keeping a copy on your phone or computer can be a great way to ensure that you can quickly access and review it.

Accept that everyone has personal struggles: No matter how happy someone seems on social media or how many accolades you have, we all go through personal struggles. Maybe the friend who seems to party all the time is struggling with depression. Maybe your successful entrepreneur cousin is struggling to find true love.

No one's life is perfect, and that's the way it is. When you accept that everyone goes through some challenges or problems, instead of feeling inferior to them, you comfort yourself whenever a comparison arises.

You will feel more comfortable in your own skin if you actively and consistently work on these strategies. Being comfortable with who you are is critical to practicing self-love and letting go of the urge to compare yourself to others. Since this is a slightly larger topic, I'll discuss it individually after discussing the barriers to self-love.

Barrier #2: People-Pleasing Behavior

A lack of self-love often leads you to look outside for love. When you look outside for love and acceptance and find it, you tend to become indebted to that person. Whoever gives you validation, appreciation, and love becomes superior to you, and you begin to please all these people.

The need to seek validation often makes you develop the habit of wanting to please people. It is similar to how low self-esteem makes you a people-pleaser and a pushover. The problem with the tendency and habit of pleasing people is that it causes you to ignore yourself and put their needs ahead of your own.

If you habitually seek the approval and respect of others, you are likely to neglect yourself when you begin to practice self-love. You may even seek their approval to love yourself as well.

This tendency to find fulfillment in pleasing others will be quite a challenge for you to face as you begin to practice self-love. The good news is that, like any other problem, it has a solution.

First, note that you have decided to put yourself first and make yourself a priority. Create an affirmation that focuses on this and practice it at least twice a day. You already know all there is to know about affirmations, so this won't be a problem.

Second, start thinking about your needs. Start by spending as little as 5 minutes thinking about your needs regarding work, health, work life, home life, family, friends, and other life disciplines. Ask yourself questions such as "What do I want?", "What is my need for love?", "What kind of work do I want to do?", "What do I like to study?", "What topics/subjects/activities excite me?", "What do I feel passionate about?", and the like.

Make a list of all these things and soon you will get more clarity about what you want.

Based on these needs, think about the things you want to do. For example, if you want to study law and not engineering like your father wants, you need to do certain things. First, you need to be sure that a career in law is right for you. You also need to gather information about the law schools you want to apply to and then send in the applications.

You also need to make sure that you meet the schools' application criteria, including having good grades. Next, you need to discuss this issue with your father and other people who are likely to have an opinion. You also need to figure out how you will stick to your decision and support yourself if your father does not support your choice.

Now you need to make time for everything you have listed. How will you do this when you are busy running errands for others, fulfilling their needs, or simply following their orders for you?

This is where you revisit your intention to prioritize yourself. Seek help from within, strengthen your intention, and then create time and space to do what you need to do for yourself.

Next, you need to create a plan to work on your goal and begin to say no to others for every unnecessary obligation, demand, or instruction they throw your way. Yes, this part will be a little more difficult than the rest, but you have it in you to cross that river, too. Just remember, you can do it!

Once you start working on these guidelines, you will empower yourself to put yourself first and overcome the challenge of pleasing others. It will take some time, but consistency will get you there 100% of the time.

Barrier #3: Over-Criticizing Yourself

If low self-esteem has been a consistent part of your life, you are probably dealing with an inner critic. As we discussed earlier, this critic will not let you acknowledge yourself. You are likely to view yourself negatively and jump at every opportunity to put yourself down.

The shame, guilt, and insecurities you nurture make you too hard on yourself. Of course, this behavior will be a big hurdle to overcome when you try to be kind and nice to yourself. Your inner critic will not easily surrender to your efforts to love yourself and raise your morale.

Even when you try to do something nice for yourself, it is likely to remind you of all your mistakes and failures, causing you to resort to being overly self-critical. So if you are trying to love yourself, this is a problem you need to work on extensively.

Here's how you can control your tendency to be too hard on yourself.

First, you need to create positive affirmations about treating yourself with kindness, love, and respect. You can also use the positive affirmations you created earlier when discussing positive self-talk.

Next, practice these affirmations as much and as often as you can.

Also, review your list of strengths daily to remind yourself of your positive qualities. This practice will strengthen your positive beliefs about yourself and encourage you to be kind to yourself when you slip into your tendency to always put yourself down.

Another thing you need to work on is self-forgiveness. Forgiving yourself is a very important part of loving yourself. One of the main reasons we tend to feel bad about ourselves is that we hold on to the grudges we have against ourselves from the past, and we feel that our lives are a mess only because of our mistakes.

Taking responsibility for your mistakes, shortcomings, and slip-ups is good, but not forgiving yourself and holding grudges against yourself will never let you move on. To work on self-forgiveness, you need to take 5 to 10 minutes out of your routine again.

During this time, write down any one thing you despise yourself for, hold a grudge against, or cannot forgive yourself for. If you feel like writing too many things, write them down.

When you have written down several things that you cannot forgive yourself for, focus on one thing that is bothering you the most right now. For example, if you hate the fact that you did not pursue your passion for theater ten years ago because you gave in to your mother's demands that you study medicine, that you lost three jobs in one year, and that you feel you are not as hardworking as your older sister, find the one thing that still bothers you the most.

Now that you have chosen one thing to focus on, think about why it hurts and makes you hate yourself. Write down your feelings. It is okay if a few tears roll down your face; let them roll down. Take several deep breaths and continue to write or record yourself as you speak.

Next, make a mental image of peace and forgiveness; if you think of it as something in white, imagine white light pouring down on you.

Close your eyes and say, "I release the hurt and hatred I have for myself and choose to forgive myself. I forgive myself. I forgive myself. I am now at peace. You can chant this affirmation all at once, or you can break it down and repeat it one sentence at a time.

After a few minutes of this practice, you will most likely feel much lighter and more relaxed than before.

Now write down your feelings and hold them. Hold this feeling for a few moments.

Make this a daily practice and soon you will find it easy to forgive yourself for all your mistakes. When you can do this, you will easily find the strength and courage to silence your inner critic and be kinder to yourself.

Also, be sure to celebrate your victories and give yourself credit for small wins throughout the day.

Also, start doing something nice for yourself at least once a week. Take a walk, paint something, bake cookies, or do anything that makes you feel happy and peaceful.

Also, every time you feel self-critical, remember this beautiful quote from Brene Brown: "Talk to yourself like someone you love. We usually have more love and kindness for others than we do for ourselves.

This behavior isn't healthy. Let's change that by talking sweetly and politely to ourselves. Whenever you feel like making fun of yourself or beating yourself up, think about how you would talk to a friend in pain. Nice, right? Use the same tone of voice as you would yourself.

You feel a little love for yourself when you start doing all these things. As a result, you also become brave enough to fight the constant urge to criticize yourself.

Barrier #4: Lack of healthy boundaries

We should treat our energy, time, and space as sacred. We must treat ourselves with respect so that others learn to behave with and around us.

Yet you are likely to lower your boundaries without self-love, or perhaps you have none; this happens primarily because you have a negative self-image. Because you don't value yourself and aren't kind to yourself, you often allow people to abuse and mistreat you.

This inability to set boundaries for yourself and others is likely to bother you when you try to prioritize yourself. If you allow others to treat you however they want, you will continue to feel this way, making it hard for you to love yourself.

You can work on this problem, too, and begin to set healthy boundaries for yourself and others.

Here are some guidelines:

First, write down the way people treat you. Go into detail about how they are harsh with you, boss you around, maybe bully you in some way, or anything else that feels like mistreatment on their part.

Next, create a mental picture and write down how you want them to respect and treat you. Again, describe it in detail.

Now consider the boundaries you need to achieve the sketch you created above.

Explain each one in detail. If it feels like too much work, focus on one boundary at a time.

Once you have a list of 4 to 5 boundaries that you need immediately so that people will treat you right, think of ways to communicate your needs to them.

Start with anyone you think might understand and try to talk to them. If they care about you, they will understand and respect that. If you are not a priority for them, take it as a sign that this person doesn't deserve your love as much as you would like to believe. You need to slowly distance yourself from such people and continue to communicate your needs to those who truly care.

As you work on setting healthy boundaries for others, you also need to set some for yourself to earn your respect and that of others; this can include things like not belittling yourself in front of others, not taking on more work than you can handle, not going overboard to make things easier for others, not being mean to others, and the like.

Think about how you allow others to disrespect and mistreat you. For example, your boyfriend may have a habit of yelling at you when he gets upset; because you have never stopped him, he continues to do this even though you would like him to stop. Even though it hurts you, you cannot stop him for fear of losing his affirmation and support.

Similarly, there may be other behaviors of your friends, family, co-workers, neighbors, social contacts, acquaintances, etc. that are uncomfortable for you. Identify them and see how you can begin to set boundaries for yourself and others.

In such cases, the biggest limit you can set for yourself is to immediately recognize these unhealthy behaviors and remind yourself how uncomfortable they are. You must first identify them as unacceptable behaviors and then communicate your concerns to the people involved.

It will take some time for all your boundaries to be in place, so be patient. Begin to work on the above practices, and keep reminding yourself that you deserve respect and love without having to get on your knees for others.

Now let us discuss other things you need to take care of in order to love yourself unconditionally.

How to Love Yourself Unconditionally

Do things that create joy in your life.

Low self-esteem and lack of self-love often lead us to engage in activities and things that others like because we seek their approval. We forget that we too have likes, interests, and dislikes.

Perhaps you like to bake, read, listen to jazz, or go to open mic sessions, but because your friends, spouse, or people you hang out with most often do not enjoy these activities, you have ignored them as well.

If you can relate to this and find little time for yourself, you have stopped living your life and are living on other people's terms. As sad as this scenario sounds, you can easily turn it into a happy one. You can do this by simply doing things you love and enjoy and by infusing your life with pure joy and peace.

Here's what you need to do.

Start by making a list of things you used to love to do but have not practiced in a long time. Things as simple as getting more rest and doing your own grocery shopping can be part of the list.

Make another list of activities that you think you might enjoy or would like to try but are somehow afraid to do. Things like trying Zumba, going on a solo trip, learning a new language, and the like can go on the list.

Now you need to carve out some time for quality "me time. Me-time refers to spending time with yourself, doing whatever you want, or even doing nothing and just exploring your thoughts. Set aside about 20 minutes a day for yourself and think about what you'd like to do. You can choose activities from the first list you prepared above.

It may seem uncomfortable at first if you have not spent time alone in a long time. But when you start doing something you like, such as painting or reading, you will enjoy being alone. The length of "me time" can also be as short as an hour or two. Experiment with this as you feel comfortable, but make it a habit to spend some time with yourself every day. Even 10 to 15 minutes of me-time on busy days can do wonders for your mental peace.

Also, occasionally do something different from your usual activities. Doing new things is magical in many ways.

First, it gets you out of your comfort zone a little bit, so you take small risks. These little experiments, like trying a French omelet, strengthen your growth mindset and gently silence your inner critic.

Second, when you try new things, you explore yourself and your interests more. Only by trying sailing can you find out if you like it or not, right?

Third, your brain fires new neural connections when you engage in new activities.

Your brain cells are stimulated by having something exciting to do, which improves your overall cognitive functioning and development.

Fourth, the excitement of doing something different is unparalleled, and it improves your emotional well-being. So pull out that second list and get involved in exciting new activities.

Learn French like you always wanted to, try strumming a guitar, take a swimming lesson, take a Pilates class, maybe sign up for a pottery class, or anything else you have always wanted to try but have been afraid to do.

As you begin to do things that bring you joy and experiment with new activities, you will feel more in control of your life. If you used to feel that your life was more about taking orders from others and doing things to please them, you will certainly feel differently now.

Take better care of yourself

Self-love is never complete without self-care. How can you say you love yourself if you do not take good care of your body? Self-care is about taking good care of your body, which includes your appearance, hygiene, sleep, and overall health.

Let me quickly walk you through these elements, their relationship to self-love and self-esteem, and how you can improve them.

Good sleep

Adults need 7 to 9 hours of sleep each night to function optimally. Lack of sleep makes us lethargic, irritable, tired, weak, stressed, and affects our cognitive development, productivity, well-being, and relationships.

If you don't get enough sleep, you may have noticed that you're easily agitated, have trouble concentrating on tasks, even slur your speech, and sometimes feel sleepy.

You should make an effort to change this if for no other reason than your lack of sleep directly affects your health and well-being.

Here's what you can do:

First, set a consistent bedtime and wake-up time that ensures you get at least 7 hours of sleep.

At least 20 minutes before going to bed, get into bed and take a few deep breaths. Calm yourself and try to fall asleep.

During the first few days, even weeks, you may toss and turn in bed and have trouble falling asleep and staying asleep. Be patient with yourself and keep lying down. Also, control your urge to sleep in when your alarm goes off when it is time to wake up. Just get up and start your day.

Make sure your room has a comfortable sleeping environment. It should not be too hot or too cold. If you prefer to sleep in a dark room, turn off the lights. If you prefer dim lighting because too much darkness can be frightening, change the lighting while you sleep. Also, make sure your mattress, pillows, and sheets are comfortable.

Avoid doing anything too exciting or stimulating just before bedtime. For example, don't exercise or do anything else that might excite you a few hours before bedtime. If you are too excited, you will find it difficult to fall asleep.

It will take some time to establish a proper sleep routine, but when you do, you will notice a significant improvement in your mood, concentration, and overall well-being.

Eat well

Eating well has a direct impact on your fitness, mood, productivity, enthusiasm, and well-being. The old adage "you are what you eat" exists for a reason.

A diet of highly processed and junk foods may seem convenient, but it is unhealthy. Because they are high in trans fats, genetically modified organisms (GMOs), artificial and processed ingredients, and chemicals, such foods make you prone to health problems such as obesity, heart problems, brain problems, diabetes, high blood pressure, and joint pain.

In addition, suppose you get sick too often or are obese. In this case, you may not feel very happy about yourself, which will affect your ability to love and accept your individuality (we will discuss this in the next chapter).

You need to be healthy and work on your diet in order to truly love yourself. Let us learn how to do this:

Analyze and write down your diet and eating habits.

If your diet consists mostly of processed fast food, you need to slowly replace it with healthy foods. These include lean meats, vegetables, especially leafy greens, fruits, organic dairy products, nuts, and plenty of water.

Slowly replace each unhealthy food in your diet with a healthy alternative.

Make sure you eat a good breakfast and drink 2 to 3 liters of water throughout the day. Staying hydrated improves your cognition, energy, stamina, concentration, and activity level. It also helps you perform your tasks better.

Start eating healthy and you will not only feel good, but you will also find it easier to manage your weight, which will improve your self-esteem.

Be physically active

Physical activity keeps you active, focused, enthusiastic, happy, fit, and energetic. And regular vigorous physical activity can help you maintain a healthy weight.

So how do you get more physically active?

Start by taking small steps. If you don't walk or move much, start walking more. Set small goals, such as taking 400 steps a day, taking the stairs instead of the elevator, and doing chores yourself instead of asking someone else.

Next, add a physical activity to your daily routine. It could be playing a sport you enjoy, walking or jogging, doing yoga, joining a gym, or doing aerobics on your own.

Start by doing this activity for 10 minutes and build up to 40 minutes over 2 to 3 months.

You can set reminders and alarms on your phone to exercise, walk, and be physically active.

Take advantage of every opportunity to get more exercise. For example, if your friends go for a hike and invite you along, join them. If your child is jumping up and down, join in. If your spouse goes for a late night walk, join them.

If you feel you need to lose weight, make a plan. Keep it realistic by spreading it out over a few months and taking daily steps to reach your goal. As you lose weight, you will start to feel healthier, which will help you feel better about yourself.

As you become more physically active, you begin to feel better from the inside out, which helps you accept your individuality.

Take care of your hygiene

You may not realize it, but ignoring your hygiene directly affects how you feel about yourself. If someone smells bad, is unpresentable, looks shabby, and isn't well dressed, you'll quickly judge that person. Similarly, you are bound to do the same with yourself.

Being unhygienic affects your self-esteem and your ability to love yourself. You automatically feel good about yourself when you are clean, neat, and presentable.

Here's what you need to do to improve your hygiene:

Start showering daily. If you can't, alternate days.

Wear a nice perfume or body spray, depending on what you like.

Moisturize your skin to keep it from becoming dry and flaky.

Keep your hair, nails, ears, and teeth clean.

Wear your hair any way you like to keep it clean. Similarly, wear whatever clothes your heart desires, but make sure they are clean.

Dress as you like, according to your style and personal preferences. Many notable public speakers and millionaire businessmen wear shorts and all-black attire to seminars. Yet people appreciate them because they look and feel clean and presentable.

Start doing these little things and you will be amazed at how good you feel about yourself.

Be sure to write in your journal every day what you have done for yourself. If you cannot do this every day, try to do it 3 to 5 times a week.

Keep track of how you have treated yourself and whether or not you now love yourself. Even if you only do the above practices a few days a week, you will notice a marked difference in your self-esteem. You will begin to like yourself more, and if you do these activities consistently, you will soon fall in love with yourself.

As you begin to like and accept yourself, you will also find within yourself the courage to accept your individuality, which is exactly the topic I am going to dive into next.

Chapter 6: Embracing Your Individuality

'True self-care is not bath salts and chocolate cake; it's choosing to build a life you don't need to escape from."

Brianna Wiest

This profound quote has been very close to my heart for quite some time. In about 25 words, Brianna West has beautifully summarized what real self-care and self-love are.

It is about choosing to live a life that you never want to run away from. A life where you accept and love yourself and choose to live on your own terms. The best way to do that is to embrace your individuality.

Let's help you understand how to own your individuality.

What is your individuality?

The Oxford Dictionary defines individuality as "the character or quality of a particular thing or person that distinguishes it from the rest.

So your individuality is everything about you, whether it's your traits, characteristics, virtues, accomplishments, or anything that gives you an edge and sets you apart from others (whether it's positive or negative).

For example, some people are introverts, which makes them enjoy their own company or that of their close friends more than being in large groups. Their introversion may be their individuality, a thing that sets them apart from others around them.

It is important to understand that individuality goes beyond the "one" thing that may be different about you compared to others. Our individuality is first and foremost being who we are and owning ourselves.

It is accepting ourselves, including our body, our face, our mind, our thoughts, our flaws, our strengths, our mistakes, our failures, our achievements, our passions, our ambitions, and everything else that makes us who we are.

I have a friend who habitually adds a pinch of honesty to everything she does and says. So when she talks about how she learned to write, she gives credit to everyone who taught her something valuable. If she had some mistakes along the way, she wouldn't hide them. She is comfortable accepting who she is and knows that she is quirky, smart, silly, and adorable. To others, this might come off as self-centered because she likes to call herself cute. But to me, this is a true example of embracing your individuality.

The truth is that each of us has something amazing, valuable, and unique to offer the world around us. The only way we can find that out is to start embracing our individuality. Unfortunately, many of us cannot do this for many reasons, including low self-esteem.

Let us examine how low self-esteem prevents you from embracing your individuality and why you need to work on embracing it.

Self-esteem and Individuality

Owning who you are and being true to yourself, no matter how quirky, weird, or different from the norm you seem, is the most rewarding way to embrace self-esteem.

When you are true to yourself, your self-worth and validation come from within, not from what others say or feel about you. It takes incredible strength to live an honest life, but it is the most rewarding experience. From the way you talk to the way you walk, from your skills to the way you use them, from the way you interact with people to your self-talk, from your behavior to your actions, everything about you creates your individuality.

Now, for many of us, owning it is difficult. You may not be comfortable with the way you act around people. You may not like being called socially awkward or introverted. Maybe you like to fake it, but every time you do it at a gathering, someone makes fun of you and you feel bad about it.

You keep expecting validation from those around you, not realizing that you need to accept yourself first. The direct or indirect behavior of others around you makes you prone to self-criticism. Gradually, you develop the habit of belittling and devaluing yourself.

Even if you don't always seek approval from others, if you don't accept your individuality, there is probably something about yourself that you are not happy with. Perhaps you are unhappy with your long nose, dislike your voice, or dislike your habit of procrastinating at work but find it difficult to change. In one way or another, there is probably something, or perhaps many things, that you disapprove of about yourself, creating self-resentment.

When self-criticism becomes the norm in your life, your inner critic gains strength, and I'm sure by now you're well aware of the effects of a strong inner critic. It further weakens your self-esteem. As your self-esteem decreases, you begin to find more faults in yourself, creating a vicious cycle!

In the midst of resentment, guilt, and bad feelings about yourself, even owning your individuality can be quite traumatizing. And if you do not own who you are, you most likely do not value yourself enough.

By embarking on the self-love journey, you can gradually begin to value yourself more. Instead of criticizing yourself for every little mistake, you begin to focus more on recognizing your strengths and finding solutions to overcome your weaknesses.

As a result, your self-esteem improves. You begin to value yourself and, over time, you can embrace your individuality. Before, you may have been too quick to criticize yourself, but now you dare to be who you are, which greatly enhances your self-worth and self-esteem.

Owning your individuality brings many other positive changes in your personality and in your life.

For example:

- You do not have to lie and make excuses to hide your shortcomings.
- You know exactly what you are good at and where you are lacking, so your sense of focus becomes clearer.
- You begin to make different choices in your life based on what you can and cannot do and what you want to do.
- You limit your interactions with people who cause you to disrespect yourself.
- You begin to build a support system of people who accept you for who you are without trying to change you.
- Instead of doing things to please people, you do what feels right for you.
- Instead of constantly rejecting the way you look, you become comfortable in your own skin.
- You begin to spend time finding your purpose in life and unlocking your spirituality.

All of these changes bring about unparalleled self-freedom: Freedom from unnecessary people-pleasing, freedom from conforming to annoying societal pressures, freedom from taking orders from others, freedom from negative thought patterns, freedom from undue stress, and freedom from being someone you are not.

Doesn't embracing your individuality sound even more exciting now? Without further ado, let me tell you what you need to do to own and truly accept yourself.

How to Own and Accept Your True Self

Accept Your Body and Yourself

Self-acceptance is critical to self-love; you cannot truly accept yourself without accepting your body. Likewise, you cannot be fully who you are until you stop shaming your body.

Unfortunately, many of us are not comfortable in our own skin. Because of societal pressures and standards of beauty, elegance, and acceptance, we tend to value certain body types and features while ignoring the rest.

If you've often found yourself belittling your physique or feeling uncomfortable about a particular body part or physical feature, it's most likely because you haven't accepted your body.

We don't understand that we are all born a certain way. Our skin color, physical features, and body types are not under our control. So if you are dark or have really small eyes, it is not your fault. There should be no shame in accepting yourself as you were born.

Things related to our bodies, such as our physique, hygiene, and self-care, are within our control. So if you are plus size but were thin when you were little, you could have controlled that. However, being plus size does not mean that you should body shame and put yourself down. Accepting yourself as you are will empower you to lose the extra weight.

Similarly, it is okay if you are messy and may look shabby to some people. You can improve, but first you must accept yourself.

To be happy with yourself, you must slowly improve this behavior of looking down on yourself and remind yourself that you are beautiful on the inside and amazing in your own way.

Here's how you can do this:

First, create positive affirmations about accepting your body and your personality. Affirmations like, "I accept my body," "I am happy with the way I look," "I am comfortable in my skin," "I love my body and the way I look" (if this feels hard to say at first, skip it and you can practice it once you start to like your body), and "I am at peace with my body. You can, of course, create more affirmations of your own; just keep them short, positive, and present-centered.

Practice these affirmations once a day or as often as possible.

Also try body scan meditation, a very gentle meditative practice that can help you accept and like your body and let go of any inhibitions you may have about your body. To practice:

Lie flat on your yoga mat, a blanket, a couch/bed, or even directly on the floor. You can even do it while sitting comfortably in a chair. Once you are seated, close your eyes and take a few deep breaths as I taught you earlier.

Next, think of any part of your body that you're not happy with. Let's take the example of your flabby belly. As you take deep breaths, bring every ounce of your attention to your belly. Gently ask yourself, "Why don't I like my belly? Acknowledge your answer and then ask yourself, "What is my flabby belly trying to tell me?

Again, make a mental note of the answer. If the answer is, "It's trying to tell me that I'm gaining weight and I need to tone it up or take better care of myself," that's fine. This time ask yourself, "Am I putting myself down or embarrassing myself about my belly?" If so, ask yourself, "Is this behavior helping me?

The answer is probably no. In this case, say to yourself, 'It is okay that I am not very happy with my belly, but I accept it and will gradually do my best to make it look and feel better. Follow this with an affirmation you created earlier and say it five times.

Gently open your eyes and tune in to your feelings. You will probably feel a little better, if not more, about your bulging belly.

Do this practice at least twice a week. You can focus on the same body part for a few weeks until you start to feel positive about it, or you can scan a different body part or feature each time.

As the weeks go by, you will stop resenting how you look and start actively working on owning it and looking and feeling better about it. At the same time, be sure to work on your hygiene, sleep, and health. When the bags under your eyes disappear and your skin feels fresh, you will automatically start to like yourself better.

Explore your individuality

You can only truly understand your individuality if you take the time to understand yourself.

To get to know your true self, begin by doing the following:

Sit in a quiet place and think about who you are.

Ask yourself questions such as, 'What best describes me?' 'What are my five greatest qualities?' 'What are my five greatest weaknesses?' 'What adjectives will I use to describe myself?' 'Is there anything that sets me apart from others?' 'If so, what is it?' 'If I am to accept my individuality, how do I define it for myself?' and the like.

Continue to examine these angels and you will soon receive answers about who you are.

After a few weeks, your report on your individuality may look like this: "I am a 39-year-old man who loves to eat and is often lazy. I am honest when I want to be, but sometimes I resort to lying. I am good at drawing and would like to pursue it. It can be different, but it will be more or less about how you see yourself. That, folks, is your individuality.

Once you get that answer, you have to tell yourself that you accept yourself. You can use affirmations like, "I accept my individuality. Although I may not be happy with certain things, I accept myself and will work to become a better version of myself. Accepting yourself and committing to be better gives you hope and makes it easier to accept your individuality.

When you begin to feel more peaceful about your individuality, you are ready to move on.

Identify Your Strengths, Then Sharpen and Use Them

Your strengths are an important part of your individuality. If you're not honing and using them well, you're wasting your potential. That's not right! You have a lot to offer the world. Here is what you need to do:

Look at your list of strengths and see how you can use them to your advantage. For example, if you're good at design, if you're undecided about a career path, or if you want to switch from your current career to something more exciting, you might want to explore that. So how can you get better at design? By taking a course, learning from online tutorials and guides, and practicing.

Now, some of your strengths may be things like character traits like sincerity and honesty. How can you use them? You can start by being more honest and dedicated in your work. Even if you don't like your current accounting job, if you do it well, you will feel accomplished if you work 7 hours straight.

With honesty, you can show it to your loved ones and yourself by being there for them and sticking to your goals. The more you think about using your positive virtues, the better ideas you will come up with to use them.

Continue to work on honing and exploring your strengths. In the process, you will discover other qualities about yourself. Think about what your heart really wants, and you will soon figure out how to use your strengths.

For example, you may discover that you have a keen interest in human psychology and are good at coaching people. These two realizations may lead you to become a life coach. Perhaps this is your true purpose in life.

I understand how hard it can feel to work on yourself, but loving yourself and embracing your individuality is love. Remember, individuality is not just about your issues and continuing to live as you are. It is also about exploring and honing your potential and becoming a better version of yourself.

Understand, Accept, and Improve Your Flaws

What are humans if not flawed? It is human to err and to lovingly accept and work on self-improvement.

To embrace your individuality, you must be comfortable with your weaknesses and work to overcome them with kindness and self-compassion.

Let me help you achieve this goal:

Go ahead and make your list of weaknesses. It is okay if it is way too long right now.

Read the list and pick 2 or 3 weaknesses that you want to start working on right away.

If you are lazy, smoke a lot, and cannot keep up with your expenses, start with the first weakness you want to overcome.

Now think about how you can stop being lazy. You will begin to get some answers. Write them down and make a plan to accomplish this goal.

Start with baby steps and small milestones, and continue to celebrate your small victories. For example, you can stop being lazy by doing whatever you need to do in the moment.

For example, if you need to change the garbage bag in the trash can, do it now instead of putting it off for two hours. You can also walk more and stay more active. Start doing these little things, and soon your laziness will be an occasional occurrence instead of a constant weakness you feel guilty about.

In the same way, start working on your weaknesses one at a time. For major weaknesses and bad habits, such as overcoming your addiction to smoking, try to find an accountability partner-someone you trust, someone you can be open with, and someone who can help you stick to your goals.

Also, quit smoking or other addictions by cutting back on them little by little. Be sure to spread out the goal of breaking such habits over a longer period of time, such as 6 to 9 months.

This strategy makes it easier to overcome big problems slowly and achieve the goal. As you begin to be kinder to yourself as you overcome your weaknesses, you will feel calmer and more at peace with yourself.

Some weaknesses or habits may not be too unhealthy, and you may feel like continuing them. For example, if you're too talkative and certain people have a problem with that, that's okay. You can gradually reduce unnecessary talking in difficult and inappropriate situations and distance yourself from the judgmental crowd. Otherwise, being talkative isn't a weakness, it's just who you are.

Similarly, if you enjoy reading erotica or making erotic pottery, so be it. It may just be who you are and nothing to feel bad about.

Letting Go of the Shiny Object Syndrome

Shiny Object Syndrome (SOS) is the tendency to keep chasing something new. It could be a new idea, opportunity, trend, career, activity, or goal. Those who have SOS do so without first evaluating that particular thing.

For example, if you change careers several times a year because you find something new or better every two months and you are rarely satisfied with your career, you probably have Shiny Object Syndrome.

Similarly, you may be chasing something else every few weeks or months. For example, you may have started out painting your room pastel blue, but after three months you decided to change it to terracotta, and after another four months you decided to change it to taupe.

Trying new things and experimenting is great. It is a good way to explore yourself. However, constantly jumping to new things without tuning into your feelings and understanding if you want to is not wise.

People with shiny object syndrome often have a habit of paying too much attention to what others expect of them. I have a friend who started freelancing about a decade ago. Let's call him Max for simplicity's sake. He started by building his skills in the area of website development.

After a few months, when he had honed his skills and could have monetized them well, he came across someone who was making a decent income from Amazon affiliate sites. Impressed by this person's income, Max started working on building his Amazon affiliate website. Six months later, when he hadn't made a dime from it, he lost hope and started doing whiteboard animation. He gave it up again when one of his colleagues told him that guest posting promised a good income.

The key takeaway from Max's story is that it is important to stick with what you believe in and give it time to see real results. Just as you cannot expect a seed to grow into a plant after one day of planting, you cannot expect an idea or effort to produce immediate results.

Moreover, you will not achieve the optimal speed and momentum you need to enjoy the journey if you keep shifting gears. To unlock true inner fulfillment, you need to stick with something consistently. To do this, it is crucial that you first fully understand what you are trying to do and also explore your feelings about this endeavor or project. If you feel connected to the activity and know that it brings inner joy, then pursue it.

You must also understand the importance of not falling victim to developing skills or pursuing ideas that society or your current environment deems appropriate and valuable. No accolade matters if you do not derive pure personal joy from it.

Make an effort to do things that are meaningful to you, that bring out the best in you, that help you feel satisfied and content, and that make you feel connected. Once you start doing this, you will begin to embrace your individuality more fully.

Every time you get excited about something, whether it is a project, an idea, a career option, or any other endeavor, tune in to your inner feelings about it. Do you find it exciting? Or is the excitement fleeting?

Write down the answers and ask yourself the same questions after 4 to 5 days. If the feeling persists, explore the possibility more deeply. For example, if you find the idea of learning AI (artificial intelligence) intriguing after a week or so, dig deeper.

Research AI and what it takes to learn it. Similarly, whatever idea or endeavor seems compelling to you, research it deeply so that you know what it takes to pursue it.

At the same time, keep checking your feelings about the venture. If they remain the same or grow even after a month of exploration, and you feel strongly that you should pursue it, then go ahead and do it. Sticking to your convictions is also part of owning your individuality. If you feel strongly about something, it is a sign that you should go on that journey.

Start working on these guidelines and you will slowly stop falling prey to the SOS. I understand that embracing your individuality can be a bit difficult, but I encourage you to give it a try.

As you progress, you will feel more in control of your life. Trust me, it will make your life a lot easier and really boost your self-esteem.

Chapter 7: The Power of Mindfulness

'Your calm mind is the ultimate weapon against your challenges. So relax.'

Bryant McGill

A calm mind is indeed a powerful weapon. But don't we already have it?

Well, not really. Just focus on how you feel and why you feel that way. Chances are that you are thinking about something other than what you are doing.

Maybe you are stuck in the thought of resenting yourself for forgetting to pack your child's lunch for school today. Or maybe you are constantly thinking about the chores you have to do for the day. Whatever it is, unfortunately, you are not in the moment and your mind is not completely still.

Only when your mind is relaxed and peaceful can you optimize your focus, health, well-being, and productivity. Mindfulness is one of the best ways to cultivate a calm mind. So what exactly is it? Why are we discussing it in a guide to boosting your self-esteem? And if it is so important, how can we practice mindfulness?

Let's find out the answers to all these questions.

Understanding Mindfulness

Mindfulness is the basic human ability to be fully present, aware of where we are and what we're doing, and not overly reactive or overwhelmed by what's happening around us.

This quote above sums up what mindfulness really is.

Mindfulness itself is a simple word. It simply means being aware of the moment you are in, all that is happening, whatever you are doing, and the space you are in.

Mindfulness is a beautiful and calm state that, when activated, allows you to let go of unnecessary worries, scary thoughts, and limiting beliefs that only hold you back. It is about becoming one with the moment to the extent that you immerse yourself in it and peacefully accept it without fighting anything that comes with it.

Let me paint a better picture with an example.

Imagine that you have just received a call from your office informing you that you have lost your job. Now, this is indeed something very upsetting. This news will certainly disturb your peace of mind. If you are not mindful of yourself, your surroundings, and the present moment, you are likely to dwell on this thought for a long time. Negative thoughts are likely to loop in your mind, making you fearful of the future.

What will happen to me now? How will I survive? How will I pay my bills? How will I pay back the loan I took from a friend? What will I do now? What if I can't get another job? Why is my life such a mess?

These and similar fears and thoughts are likely to bombard you. You may also feel sad for days on end.

On the other hand, when you enter a state of mindfulness, you are likely to behave differently than in the scenario described above. Yes, you will be upset by the news. You may even cry, feel guilty, and even blame yourself for a while, a reaction most people would have in an adverse situation.

After a few moments, however, you will calm down and accept it as something that has happened and there is not much you can do about it. You will then shift your focus to solving the problem: finding another job and getting out of debt.

Let's take another example.

Suppose you are stuck in a long traffic jam for 2 hours. You are likely to get frustrated, slam the steering wheel, lose your temper, and maybe even curse. If you are mindful, you accept this as a part of life.

Now that you are in this situation, think about how you can be calmer and accepting. You can play songs, listen to motivational lectures, or practice affirmations.

Consciously or unconsciously, many of us live in the past or the future and rarely in the present. We're either rehashing moments that have happened or worrying about what's coming next. Don't get me wrong, there is nothing wrong with recalling and reminiscing about your memories, both good and bad. Going down memory lane and reminiscing about the good old days is fun and it lifts your spirits.

It is also human and perfectly acceptable to revisit unhappy memories from time to time. However, constantly living in the past, whether happy or sad, keeps you from fully embracing and using the moment.

Similarly, if you only worry about the future, you will remain in a constant state of worry and not take action in the here and now.

Mindfulness teaches you to accept the moment nonjudgmentally and peacefully, without attaching specific emotions. This approach helps you let go of your worries, concerns, and even heightened emotions of joy and excitement.

Often, when we are overwhelmed with joy, we tend to make impulsive and not very fruitful decisions. For example, you may move in with someone you have been dating for a week because you are too in love or too happy to have found someone, only to realize a month later that you made a bad decision.

Mindfulness allows you to overcome this weakness and can trigger many beautiful changes in your life.

The relationship between mindfulness and self-esteem

Mindfulness and self-esteem have a very strong and directly proportional relationship. The two influence each other.

Let's explore this a little deeper.

The main reason I talk about mindfulness in this self-esteem blueprint is because it helps you become more aware of your thoughts and then control how they affect you instead of letting them control you.

Often, negative thoughts creep into our minds without our realizing it; this happens because we are unaware and mostly live in the past or future.

When you become more mindful, you can quickly recognize negative thoughts before they wreak havoc in your mind; you can recognize a weed just as it is about to grow and pull it up. With no weeds to pollute your mind, you can sow the seeds of positivity in your mind and make them fertile. The result? Flowers of positivity bloom and you begin to live a good life.

So, when you are mindful of your thoughts, you are more aware of what you are thinking. Whenever an upsetting thought enters your mind or begins to take hold, you can easily recognize it, calm it down, and replace it with something more meaningful. Naturally, this practice improves your sense of self-worth.

Second, mindfulness allows you to recognize your strengths and weaknesses, find ways to use the former constructively, and work on the latter more positively. Again, this increases your self-esteem.

In addition, mindfulness keeps you from constantly rehashing your past and living in a state of panic, imagining the worst possible outcomes in the future. You focus more on doing what is important right now, even if it is just being quiet and not thinking too actively.

As you live better in the present, you understand it and your unimaginably amazing power better. As a result, you begin to use it better. As a result, your self-esteem increases.

I have broken down the many other positive improvements that mindfulness brings to your life so that you can easily grasp this process.

- You become more optimistic and positive about difficult situations.
- You begin to think outside the box when you are stuck in a rut.

- Instead of beating yourself up, you accept that certain things are bound to happen.
- Instead of falling into the "negativity" trap, you focus more on finding solutions.
- You accept that your past is gone, that the future is uncertain and out of your control, and pay more attention to embracing the present.
- You become more peaceful and find it easier to pay attention to yourself, your life, and your needs.

- As you become more relaxed and happier, you gain the strength to focus more on your relationships.

With all of these positive changes happening in your life, it will naturally improve.

So how can you practice mindfulness?

How to Practice Mindfulness

While there are many ways to practice mindfulness, here are a few simple ones.

Relax and do nothing

Mindfulness is about training yourself to become one with the present moment. Once you get the hang of it, you are always in a state of mindfulness, whether you are doing something or not.

The "relax and do nothing" approach teaches you just that.

Sit or stand anywhere for just 30 seconds.

Set a timer for 30 seconds, and when it starts, do nothing.

For those 30 seconds, don't focus on any thought that comes into your head.

You don't need to take a deep breath; just do whatever feels natural.

You may feel like fidgeting, moving around, scratching your head, or checking your phone. In those moments, tell yourself that the goal is to relax and do nothing, and you'll find it a little easier to control the urge.

Once you stop fighting these temptations, getting through those 30 seconds will be a breeze.

It will take some time to do nothing, even for 30 seconds, so cut yourself some slack. Don't immediately expect yourself to be mentally still, even for 10 seconds. But it will happen if you are consistent with the practice.

Each time your mind wanders off in thought, acknowledge that active thinking has occurred and you need to go back to your practice of just doing nothing, not even active thinking. You will get there, trust me.

It will take you a few days to get the hang of the practice, so be patient with yourself. Journaling the experience (even recording yourself talking about it) will help you stay consistent with the practice and keep track of your performance and progress.

Mindfulness Meditation: Easy Version

Meditation is a healthy practice that allows you to focus on what is important and let go of everything else. It helps you develop mindfulness and the ability to live in that state. Eventually, when you become quite good at meditation, you are always in a state of mindfulness. That's when you are always meditating and always mindful.

Mindfulness meditation is about training your mind to focus on any one thing. It could be a thought you want to explore, the work you are doing, or just the moment.

There are many ways to meditate, but I'm going to teach you one of the easiest ways to meditate: mindfulness meditation by focusing on an object.

Choose any object you want to focus on. It can be a table, a vase on the table, your hand, a book, a leaf, a plant by the window, or just your breath.

Sit, stand, or lie down in whatever way is most comfortable for you. It is better to sit, because it can be a challenge to stand up straight while focusing for 5 minutes, and it can be a little difficult to do it lying down, because you may fall asleep. Take a few deep, cleansing breaths.

Set your timer for about 2 minutes. Yes, we will start with baby steps and slowly increase the duration to about 15 minutes within 2 to 3 weeks.

As you feel more relaxed, slowly focus on the object you have chosen to meditate on. For example, suppose you focus on your breath and meditate on a vase on the table.

As you focus on your breath, take a deep breath and notice how the air enters your body through your nose. Stay with it and then observe it as it moves inside your body and gently out through your mouth as you exhale.

Stay with it for about 2 minutes. If at any point your mind wanders off in thought, acknowledge this and bring your attention back to your breath. You can even count it out loud to stay focused.

If you are mindful of a vase, observe it from top to bottom. Focus on the color, the shade, the shape of the vase, any pattern on it if it is patterned or has any design, and how it appears on the table. Thoughts like 'Why am I doing something so meaningless?' 'Why is it important?' 'Is the vase ugly or pretty?' and the like may come and go in your mind. Ignore them: keep watching the vase.

When the timer beeps, take another deep breath, whether you are observing your breath or an inanimate object such as a vase.

Now think about how you feel at this moment. You probably feel lighter than before. You may feel a little fuzzy or a little confused, and that's okay. This is just the beginning. It will take some time for your mind to get used to focusing on one thing because it hasn't done this for a long time.

Make it a habit to practice this technique for 2 minutes once a day. In about a week, you will begin to meditate better and enjoy it more.

Slowly increase the length of your practice to 15 minutes by adding a minute or two each week.

Do your chores mindfully

Once you become more mindful of your thoughts and breaths, take that awareness to the next level and infuse it into everything you do. From writing to reading, cooking to driving, preparing a report to simply walking, perform every task, from the smallest to the largest, with moment-to-moment awareness. You will be amazed at how fun, meaningful, and exciting everything becomes.

Here's how you need to work on your chores:

If you are reading a book, read slowly and calmly.

As you read, focus on each word and process it completely before moving on to the next.

When you finish a sentence, think about what it means. When you fully understand the meaning, move on to the next sentence.

Every time you drift off, say out loud, "I'm just reading and concentrating.

Continue to read in this way for as long as you intend to read.

Similarly, when eating, take small bites, chew them completely, enjoy the taste, and then take another bite.

When you cook, immerse yourself in the experience by concentrating on the aroma of the food, the way the curry bubbles, the way you add the spices, and so on. The idea is to do everything with complete concentration.

Avoid multitasking while doing something. Yes, multitasking can sometimes be a lifesaver, but do not make it a routine.

The more you multitask, the more your focus decreases. It then becomes difficult to concentrate on one thing and do it well with full concentration; this also adds to your stress level.

High stress levels make it easier to fall prey to unhealthy thought patterns that negatively affect your self-esteem. This is one of the most beneficial stress-busting techniques you can practice to curb your chronic stress and stay happy, so avoid multitasking and keep building your self-esteem.

Mindful listening and speaking

Mindful listening and mindful speaking are two extraordinary practices that can make your life simple and easy if you make them a habit.

We usually listen and speak based on our preconceived notions and in a hurry. So if you have heard that those who consume a lot of alcohol are likely to behave erratically, you may not listen carefully to an alcoholic friend and ignore even his wise words. Similarly, if you do not like a co-worker, you may not listen carefully to his advice, even though it may be beneficial to you.

Similarly, when we speak, we may be judgmental and not speak with an unbiased and conscious state of mind. As a result, we sometimes say hurtful things to others and project our bitterness onto others.

Mindful speaking and mindful listening are two practices that, if you make a habit of them, can bring many positive improvements to your life.

For example:

You begin to listen more patiently to loved ones to strengthen your bond with them.

You begin to speak mindfully to others, which helps you speak kindly and courteously. As a result, you become easy to be around and begin to feel good about yourself. As a result, your self-esteem increases.

You begin to take criticism graciously and focus more on the positive aspects of the criticism you receive. Being receptive to constructive criticism allows you to think and act positively and harness the power of positive criticism.

You will stop making unfounded assumptions on your own and think more mindfully.

You let go of your preconceptions about different ideas, concepts, practices, and people. For example, you may have believed that 'homosexuality' was unacceptable or bad. However, as you become a more mindful listener, you may see it more openly and nonjudgmentally.

You become more accepting of new ideas, concepts, and experiences, so you experiment with new things. Even if you don't experiment, you become more open to different things that expand your horizons.

You begin to listen carefully to your thoughts, building the strength to keep the thoughts that are important and to reframe the hurtful ones.

As you begin to speak more mindfully, your self-talk becomes more positive and constructive, increasing your self-esteem.

So, how do you build the ability to listen and speak mindfully?

Whenever you listen to something, let go of the need to label and attach any judgment.

Focus on each word you hear and try to make sense of it calmly. If you cannot do this immediately, do it later. You will probably understand it better later and accept its truth.

Think deeply about any suggestion, advice, or criticism before you react. You may feel the urge to respond immediately to some criticism. For example, your friend tells you that you need to work on your "can't-do" attitude and be more responsible. This advice and criticism may offend you, and you may even feel like yelling something hurtful, rude, or mean. Take a deep breath and suppress that urge.

Next, politely thank the person for the suggestion/criticism. Later, when you are alone, think about the criticism. Look at it from different angles and see if there is any truth to it. Examine yourself in a session of relaxing mindfulness-based meditation.

Does anyone think you have a negative attitude? If the answer is "yes," consider how it affects your life and its various aspects. You are likely to analyze those aspects more dispassionately and accept the advice. If you do this every time someone gives you advice or criticism, you will begin to take it constructively. If you agree to use the criticism in your life, thank the person later.

If, after your analysis, you feel that the criticism is not worthwhile, let it go. There is no point in holding on to something that does not help you.

At the same time, let go of any bitter feelings you may have developed toward the critic. Holding on to these feelings will only create more bitterness within you and, in one way or another, weaken your self-esteem.

Start working with these guidelines and soon mindfulness will become a part of your listening and speaking practice.

As you become more mindful, you will remain calmer than usual. This sense of calmness will help you manage stress even better. Stress is a big offender when it comes to self-esteem, and equipping yourself with the ability to combat it is crucial to continually building your self-esteem.

Let's talk more about it in the following chapter, *"Managing Stress for Better Self-Esteem."*

Chapter 8: Managing Stress for Better Self-Esteem

"Stress is like spice: In the right proportion, it enhances the flavour of a dish. Too little produces a bland, dull meal;
too much may choke you."

Donald Tubesing

Let us now move on and talk about stress, its effect on your self-esteem, and how to manage it to empower and strengthen your sense of self-worth.

The Physics of Understanding Stress

Usually, we use stress to refer to the feeling we experience whenever we go through tension, problems, or an unpleasant and overwhelming situation.

However, in its truest sense, stress is your body's reaction to anything it finds different and unusual from routine. Does that mean an exciting or potentially positive situation can trigger stress in our body? Well, yes! I'll explain this later, too. First, I want you to comprehend what stress is.

Any time your body goes through a challenging or different situation, your brain receives the 'stress' signal and sets off a certain response known as the 'fight, flight, or freeze' mechanism.

This mechanism triggers a series of physiological changes in your body that help you better cope with the seemingly stressful situation. The body releases certain hormones, such as adrenaline and cortisol, into your bloodstream to bring about physical changes and trigger feelings like excitement and worry.

The physiological changes include rapid heartbeat, profuse sweating, increased blood flow, and tightening of the limb muscles. This mechanism, also known as the 'stress response,' makes you fight the situation, flee it to look for ways to escape it, or freeze as if becoming completely numb.

The flight mechanism happens in extreme scenarios. For instance, if you see a tiger in front of you roaring crazy and trying to gobble you up, you might freeze.

Let us go back to the fight-or-flight reactions. Both these responses help you handle an upsetting, stressful situation effectively. For instance, when stuck in a traffic jam, you will likely find a detour or calm yourself down and endure it. If you see a snake in your toilet, you will become more alert, try to run from it, or seek a way to get it out of the toilet patiently.

Now, I have discussed upsetting scenarios in terms of experiencing stress, but I also mentioned how stress can seep inside your system when something exciting or positive happens.

Imagine your boss just told you that you will be the team leader, giving you a great salary raise; this is a very happy and exciting occurrence that comes with responsibilities and challenges.

Also, it is different from what you go through in your normal routine. Your stress response becomes active, and the adrenaline rush in your body makes you feel invigorated and apprehensive. This stress you experience in positive situations is known as 'positive stress' or 'eustress.'

So, stress may seem like a negative phenomenon, but it is quite helpful in many situations.

But how does it impact your self-esteem?

The Impact of Stress on Self-Esteem

Experiencing stress occasionally is normal. However, if you are consistently stressed, that is a problem because adrenaline and cortisol keep flowing in your blood and circulating throughout your body, signaling your brain that you are in a stressful situation even when you are not.

Naturally, when you feel stressed, your thoughts lean more toward the negative side. You keep feeling negative about yourself and your life, reinforcing your limiting beliefs. Hence, you quickly blame yourself in a stressful situation, believe you cannot do anything right, and feel a sense of inadequacy pumping into your system all the time.

When such feelings and thoughts become a norm, you keep lowering your value and adversely affecting your self-esteem. But stress can also positively impact your self-esteem, too, at times.

When you experience positive situations where you feel stressed, you will likely boost your morale by thinking and saying positive things. For instance, in the picture painted above where your boss says you are the team leader, you are likely to tell yourself that while the responsibility is huge, it is also a great opportunity to prove your mettle and remind yourself of how you can succeed.

When you believe you can do something, your self-esteem increases. Yes, it is basically about how you perceive a situation. If you train yourself to stay optimistic even in upsetting situations, you will use your stress positively and continue to supply yourself with positive thoughts.

As a result, your self-esteem once again improves. So yes, if you know how to combat and handle stress effectively, you can reframe negative situations and keep them from lowering your self-esteem.

Now that we have established the connection between self-esteem and stress, let us discuss managing stress while increasing your self-esteem.

In most cases, the stress accumulates inside us due to a lack of fulfillment, self-love, self-care, and a negative mindset. So, when you start working on the guidelines pertinent to these issues discussed previously, much of your stress will automatically reduce.

Let me share some more stress-reduction strategies with you so you can use a handful of tools to manage your issue effectively.

Stress-breaking Strategies That Work

Identify Your Stressors

It is easier to solve any problem when you know its root cause; the same is true for stress. In order to successfully manage your stress, you must first identify the stressors.

A stressor triggers your stress response and makes you feel stressed. You can have one or more stressors in different situations and even in the same or similar situations. It is important to identify them so that you know what is causing you to lose your calm, worry, and become exhausted. Knowing the stressors allows you to develop coping mechanisms and use effective stress-reduction tactics.

Here is what you can do:

Mindfully observe yourself in various situations, especially during moments of anxiety, nervousness, and frustration.

When you feel yourself experiencing these or similar feelings, take a break from whatever you are doing and sit with your feelings.

Try to rewind the scenario and get back to where it all started. If you feel emotionally overwhelmed, think about what happened 10 minutes ago and then rewind (in your mind) 5 to 10 minutes to the point where something upsetting happened. Perhaps you had an unpleasant interaction with the cashier at the grocery store where you did your shopping an hour ago that is still fresh in your mind.

Be sure to <u>write down your stressors</u> as you identify them.

Remember, a stressor can be anything. From an increasing workload, to harsh conversations, to rude behavior, to being late for work, to financial pressures, to rising inflation, to being mistreated by a loved one, to not feeling accomplished, and so on.

As you begin to identify your stressors, you will better understand what doesn't work. Please experiment with different things to deal with these stressors. The techniques I've discussed above and those I'll share in this chapter are all great ways to manage stress.

As you work on them, you will find that some strategies work for you and some do not. The idea is to stick with the helpful ones and use them to build your "stress management toolkit" so that you are ready to curb your stress before it gets out of hand.

Slow down and take it easy

Modern life is busy. That is now a fact. Another fact is that we need to slow down and take it easy from time to time.

One of the main reasons you may feel so exhausted is that you are going through a lot of stressful situations. This happens mainly because you do not allow yourself to relax and you are always on the go or doing something that makes you feel overwhelmed, tired and stressed. This stress builds up and makes you feel overwhelmed all the time.

As important as it is to take care of all your responsibilities, chores, and work, taking a break and not doing anything big that requires your full attention is crucial to your personal well-being.

Here is a process you can try:

After 2 to 3 hours of consecutive work on your most important tasks, take a 15-minute break and do nothing but lie down on a couch or sit in a chair. Close your eyes and allow yourself to relax by thinking and doing nothing.

Second, at the end of the day, spend 15 to 30 minutes doing some relaxing and enjoyable activity. This could be playing a sport such as badminton or basketball, swimming if possible, reading a book, listening to music, or sipping coffee in your garden. The idea is to do something that helps you relax after a busy day.

If possible, set aside one day a week or month to do absolutely nothing. Try to get all your work-related tasks done before that day, so there is no pressure to meet a deadline. As for food, do not cook that day; order in or get take-out. For all other family and personal chores, do them before that day.

On this day, do whatever your heart desires. Binge-watch shows on Netflix, meet with friends, watch social media videos, engage in a hobby or activity that you enjoy, or lie in bed and rest. If it is difficult to take a whole day for yourself, relax for a few hours. Even that can be enough.

Start slowing down and relaxing a little more; you may be surprised at how calm you feel.

Eat well to reduce stress

If stress has become a regular part of your life, pay attention to your diet. Certain foods increase our stress, so eating them often could explain why you feel anxious and overwhelmed all the time.

Foods that contain refined carbohydrates and added sugars, such as white bread, pasta, and sugary sweets, raise blood sugar levels. As your blood sugar rises, your body works harder to produce insulin to regulate it. You go through a crash, which has a domino effect on the various hormones in your body. One of the results of this process is increased levels of cortisol, the infamous stress hormone. With more cortisol in your bloodstream, you feel more stressed.

In addition, over-consumption of caffeinated beverages increases your stress levels. Caffeine overstimulates our natural stress response and disrupts sleep. As a result, you find it difficult to relax and feel exhausted.

Fast and processed foods and all foods high in trans fats also negatively affect your stress levels by causing inflammation, which upsets your body and causes stress. Also, these foods have fats that are harder to break down, so your body cannot use them immediately for fuel and stores them for a while. When your body has to work a little harder, it feels more stressed.

In addition, overeating increases your stress levels because your body has to work harder to break down the food.

You can manage stress better by limiting your intake of the above foods and eating according to your needs. Before eating more, check with your body to see if you are hungry, and focus more on eating healthier foods as discussed in the book.

Also, certain foods relieve stress, so include them in your diet to control your stress levels.

High-quality proteins have neurotransmitters and hormones that make up your stress response, so eating foods rich in high-quality proteins, such as eggs and fatty fish like tuna and salmon, will regulate your stress response and create a sense of balance in your body.

Teas contain L-theanine, an amino acid that relaxes your body and stimulates your brain to produce anxiety-reducing chemicals. So, drinking teas like peppermint and chamomile is a great way to get rid of that annoying stress you keep experiencing.

In addition, fermented and probiotic foods like Greek yogurt and sauerkraut balance the bacteria in your digestive tract. Serotonin, an important mood-boosting hormone, is a byproduct of the gut, so when it is balanced, it is easier to fight stress and feel happier.

Foods rich in magnesium also reduce stress because magnesium helps improve sleep quality and reduce anxiety. Leafy greens, dark chocolate, and salmon are high in magnesium, so add these foods to your diet. Go easy on the dark chocolate, as too much of it can also increase your stress levels.

Research shows a link between stress and vitamin D deficiency. People with anxiety, depression, and stress often have low vitamin D levels. The exact link between stress and vitamin D is still unknown, but eating foods high in vitamin D, such as cheese and eggs, will help balance your stress levels.

Now that you know the link between stress and foods, steer clear of the stress-inducing foods and load up on the stress-busting ones.

Stay active to stay happy

Physical activity and exercise are known ways to reduce stress. They improve the production of happy hormones like serotonin, which helps you feel calmer and happier and keeps stress at bay.

Make some time for physical activity and exercise in your routine, and you'll feel more in control of your stress.

Plan accordingly

Are you always late for work, always missing deadlines, and always trying to get so much done in so little time? This is probably why you feel so overwhelmed. A good way to manage this stress is to plan ahead. If you are prepared to take care of your tasks in advance, you can avoid the stress of not completing tasks, missing deadlines, and being late.

Here is a process you can follow:

Set your watch about 10 minutes ahead of time. Soon you will be getting ready for work, meetings, get-togethers, and other activities on time and arriving early or on time.

Plan your tasks for the next day the night before so that when you wake up the next day, you know what to do and don't have to spend time planning things.

Delegate non-essential tasks to others or get help with them. If checking emails and responding to them takes up a lot of your time and leaves you with less time to work on important tasks, hire a VA. If laundry is time-consuming, hire a laundry service to wash your clothes.

Keep a to-do list of your tasks for the day, one on your phone and one printed out and taped to your desk. This will help you stay on top of your tasks and avoid missing important ones.

Analyze your tasks for the entire month and make some lists. One could be for the big tasks, one for the routine tasks, and one for the passion projects or other projects you want to do but never find the time for. Schedule the big ones for the first two weeks of the month, delegate the trivial ones, and you will have some time to take care of your passion projects.

If you have an event or activity that requires you to travel, plan for it at least 2-3 weeks in advance so you are ready when you arrive. While packing the essentials can be done a day or two before you travel, you can buy any items you need, such as a power bank.

Practice better time management

Lack of efficient time management is often a major stressor in itself. If you do not manage your time effectively, you will always have a full plate, ready to burst at any moment.

On the other hand, when you manage your time better, you complete your tasks on time, resulting in less stress and better self-esteem.

Here is how you can practice excellent time management:

Break down the big, overwhelming tasks into smaller, more manageable segments. If you are writing a project report, break it down into parts such as research, findings, analysis, results, goals for the future, and so on.

Then, give each segment a reasonable amount of time and a deadline, and start working on each small task.

For example, you might spend 3 hours on research on Monday, 2 hours on analysis on Tuesday, and so on. When you break huge tasks down into less overwhelming tasks, you find it easier to stay on top of them and get them done on time.

Try the "eat an ugly frog at the beginning of the day" approach for your most challenging tasks. The ugly frog is an analogy for the difficult tasks, and eating it refers to working on them first thing each day.

As you plan your tasks for the next day, identify the big ones, especially those that you have been putting off for a long time, mainly because they seem challenging.

The next day, do a little meditation and then eat the ugliest frog of the bunch. Yes, the task may seem difficult at first, but once you start working on it for 10 to 15 minutes, you will get in the groove and complete it, or at least a big chunk of it. The sense of accomplishment and relaxation you will feel at the end will be amazing. It will also boost your motivation, allowing you to work more effectively and efficiently on other tasks.

If procrastination gets the better of you, pick a task you can do right now and get to it. If it seems difficult to work on, set a timer for 2 or 5 minutes. We call this the "2 or 5 minute" strategy; it helps you get started on a task without delay. Because 2 or 5 minutes is not a very long time, working on something for that long does not seem too difficult. Of course, when you start a task, you get the urge to do as much of it as possible, which keeps you going.

Try these time management hacks and soon you will see your productivity increase to a great extent. Good productivity reduces your stress and boosts your self-esteem.

Stop chasing perfectionism

Stress also comes from constantly chasing perfectionism and wanting to do everything just right. Perfectionism is a myth. No matter how hard you try, there will always be something you can do better or something you can't do.

The constant desire for "perfectionism" only weighs you down. You feel inadequate when you cannot do something perfectly as planned, which triggers your self-critical thoughts and diminishes your self-esteem.

What's the solution? Settle for good enough.

Settling for good enough means acknowledging what you have done that is relevant to a particular task, giving yourself credit, celebrating the small victory, looking for areas of improvement, and moving on.

This makes you feel more accomplished and less stressed.

Here's how to practice this process:

As you begin a task, affirm a positive productivity suggestion and acknowledge yourself. You can say, "I'm starting my paper, and I'm going to do it well.

Give yourself a specific time frame. For example, if you are working on your thesis and it is due in 3 months, the deadline can be a week before.

Break it down into parts and give each part a timeframe.

Start working on it step by step, and make sure you do it deliberately.

Once you have worked on a particular task for its allotted time in a day, acknowledge and appreciate yourself for working hard.

Next, analyze where you could have done better and create a strategy for better results next time.

Apply this approach to your tasks, whether it is cooking, cleaning the house, doing an office task, or even a passion project like taking a portrait. Over time, your stress levels will drop significantly, making you more focused and happier.

Surround Yourself with Supportive, Positive People

Sometimes the stress you feel doesn't come from your actions, but from what you pick up from those around you.

Being around people who bring you down by reminding you of your weaknesses or past mistakes, and those who are ungrateful and generally always complaining about everything, will naturally add to your stress.

The anecdote to this problem is to replace them with happier, more optimistic and uplifting people who spread good vibes and leave you feeling refreshed and motivated.

Analyze the people in your social circle, especially those with whom you spend the most time on a daily basis.

Now think about how each of them makes you feel. Write down the answers and reflect on how the negative influences of one or another are keeping you from strengthening your self-esteem.

Slowly distance yourself from these people. It will be hard, but you can do it gradually. If you see a friend (whom you consider a negative influence in your life) every week, go two weeks without seeing him, and then schedule a meeting if he insists.

In the meantime, focus more on being around people who lift your spirits and encourage you to improve. Meet, talk, and engage with them whenever you can. Happiness hormones will begin to surge in your body and lower your stress levels.

The more you limit your interactions with the negative and increase your engagement with the positive, the calmer you will feel.

I have discussed with you several stress-busters that can improve your quality of life. Start working on these practices and take your happiness to a new level.

Chapter 9: The Importance of Healthy Relationships in Self-Esteem

'The more you love yourself, the more love you have to give to others. It's a beautiful cycle of positivity.'

Anonymous

Love is only increased when you share it with others, and when you learn to truly love yourself, you become better at loving others. It's very important to have the ability to love, respect, and care for others, because that's how you build healthy and rewarding relationships.

Humans are social animals. We thrive on quality human connection, even with just a few people. Even if you think you can survive alone, which you can, to thrive in this world and be happy at your core, you need beautiful relationships. That is the focus of this chapter.

Building healthy relationships also has an obvious and significant impact on your self-esteem. Let us talk a little more about this, and then guide you on how to build meaningful relationships to live a happy, balanced, and prosperous life.

The Relationship-Self-Esteem Connection

Your self-esteem and your interpersonal relationships are closely related. How you behave in a relationship sets a standard for how other people treat you, and their treatment strongly affects how you perceive yourself and, consequently, your self-esteem.

For example, if you are kind to your friends, they will be kind to you and naturally respect you. You feel valued by receiving kindness and respect from your friends, which improves your self-esteem.

On the other hand, if you are mean to someone, there is a good chance that they will return the favor. You may disapprove of their behavior, but either way, it will make you see yourself in a dim, dark light, resulting in a low self-esteem.

In addition, if you have the people-pleasing tendencies discussed earlier, you are likely to allow others, especially your loved ones, to walk all over you. They may still love you, but if you occasionally give in to their needs, they may barely listen to you and even disregard your feelings.

Have you ever faced situations where your spouse did not care what you thought and did what you asked so as not to leave you feeling disrespected and hurt? Or times when your friends kept pushing you away, but ran to you every time they needed a favor?

Yes? Then you know how bad it feels when someone treats you that way. Such behaviors make you feel violated and can negatively affect your sense of adequacy and worth. The result is a dwindling sense of self-worth.

But you do not want to be treated that way, do you? You want to give pure love and receive pure love in return. You deserve that.

Start working on your relationships to make that happen. The first step is to understand the true meaning of a healthy relationship.

Understanding the Meaning of Healthy Relationships

A healthy relationship, whether with your parents, siblings, boyfriend/girlfriend, spouse, children, coworkers, or anyone else, is built on trust, love, respect, open communication, faith, and care.

Healthy relationships are never one-way. They are a two-way phenomenon, requiring effort, compromise, and care on both sides.

Healthy relationships also operate on the basis of equality. While there may be times when one party gets priority and the other gets more favors, unfair treatment, self-centeredness, and power imbalances do not exist in a healthy relationship.

Both people, especially the two people in an intimate, loving relationship, respect each other's space, independence, ability to make decisions, and ability to make decisions together.

Here are the primary **basic characteristics of a healthy relationship:**

You and the other person respect each other's space and privacy. Whether it is your children, a dependent sibling, your parents, or your partner, you do not demand that they be with you all the time and expect them to do the same for you.

You and the other person in a relationship, especially an intimate one, feel safe in each other's company. Children should not feel threatened by you, and you should not allow them to violate your sense of respect. Similarly, you and your partner should not feel uncomfortable, uneasy, or coerced in a relationship.

You respect each other's wishes and take care to meet each other's needs.

You feel free to make your own decisions, but you also know the importance of sharing them with the right person. You and your partner need to trust each other's decision-making abilities and listen to each other, especially if the suggestion is beneficial.

You do not force your decisions on your loved ones; instead, you allow them to decide for themselves and make their own mistakes. You deserve that they show you the same respect.

You feel comfortable sharing your concerns, feelings, and opinions about various things in your relationships, and you encourage others to do the same.

For example, you do not avoid your parents when they express concerns about your work; you listen patiently. At the same time, you should be able to discuss your opinions about your career with them without being judged, frowned upon, or insulted in any way.

As for children, you need to understand their generational characteristics, encourage them to talk about their feelings, and welcome their input in decisions that involve them.

As for your relationship with your partner, you and your partner should be able to talk about your feelings, emotions, hesitations, fears, doubts, insecurities, and expectations of each other without feeling ridiculed or disrespected.

You and your partner should spend quality time together and apart. You and your partner should hang out together and spend time alone with friends when you and your partner feel like it.

Similarly, you should spend quality time with your children and family and give them the confidence to hang out with their friends without spying on them.

Do not always interfere with each other's privacy and money matters; this is especially important for your relationship with your partner. While sharing your money-related decisions and activities is nice for both of you, it should not be an obligation.

At the same time, it is important to share this information if a financial activity affects the other person's well-being. For example, your spouse needs to know if you are considering investing $10,000 in stocks.

You handle conflicts amicably, without overriding the other person's opinion and without letting them disrespect yours. You find a middle ground in any situation to restore peace and love.

These qualities may seem unimaginable if you have not had healthy relationships. But the truth is, a healthy relationship includes all of them; this happens best when you build the relationship on the right foundation.

The Foundation of Healthy Relationships

Healthy relationships are built on a healthy foundation, which includes:

Boundaries: It is crucial to set healthy boundaries in any relationship in order to feel respected and loved, and to give love and respect to the other person.

Trust: Both parties need to have faith in each other and their abilities. You should trust the other person to be faithful to you and to be able to make their own decisions. And they should trust you in return.

Strong, open communication: Open and strong communication is a crucial ingredient in any thriving relationship, especially one you share with your partner, children, parents, and close friends. People in a relationship should be able to share their feelings, even when they disagree. Communication must be free of judgment, disrespect, and hurt.

Consent: Eliciting the other person's consent is essential to the growth of the relationship. Any coercion or compulsion should not exist in a relationship or it will weaken over time.

Love and Care: No relationship grows better without love and caring. You and the other person must show care, affection, and admiration for each other in order to value each other.

When you build your relationships on a core foundation of these ingredients, they become healthy, happy, meaningful, and powerful.

Now, let's talk about how to do this.

Setting Healthy Boundaries in a Relationship

Healthy boundaries in a relationship aren't walls that separate you from your loved ones. Different rules based on understanding and acceptance allow you to set certain criteria for how others should behave with you in different relationships.

From giving people in a relationship more space and independence, to respecting each other's privacy, to communicating with love and respect, boundaries help bring and restore balance, equality, respect, and trust in a relationship.

Suppose you often feel hurt in your relationships, and your loved ones do not respect you, or perhaps you hurt them in some way. Then it is time to set some healthy and meaningful boundaries in your relationships.

With boundaries in place, you feel more autonomous and can reduce your codependent habits. They also set expectations for how you will interact with others and teach others how to do the same. They also give you a sense of empowerment and determine your emotional and physical comfort.

In addition, healthy boundaries help you and your loved ones clarify the different responsibilities that each of you must assume. You can also easily understand and separate your needs, desires, feelings, and thoughts from those of others. As a result, your self-esteem and the quality of your relationships improve.

Without boundaries, your relationships tend to become unsatisfying and toxic. You feel taken advantage of, and your emotional well-being suffers. The importance of healthy boundaries in your life is clear.

Let us look at how you can create healthy boundaries in your relationships.

First, you need to identify what you want and need in your relationships. The best way to do this is to take a journal and write down some of the most important relationships in your life in the name of the person with whom you share that bond.

For example, there may be columns such as "My relationship with my mother 'Amanda,' 'My relationship with my spouse 'John/Rachel,' 'My relationship with my son 'Adam,' 'My relationship with my best friend 'Daniella,' and so on. You can also create general columns such as 'Relationship with Parents', 'Relationship with Children', etc.

It is best to start with each relationship that you want to improve and that needs healthy boundaries.

Now you need to figure out what you want in that relationship. Whether it is platonic, romantic, or biological, it is difficult to get your needs met if you are not aware of them in the first place. A good place to start is to reflect on your beliefs and values.

Ask yourself questions such as 'What behaviors upset me?' 'What qualities do I want to see in this relationship with this person?' 'What kinds of things make me feel happy and fulfilled?' 'What qualities do I want to see in the other person? ' 'How do I like to spend my time alone?' 'What expectations do I have of this person and what expectations can he/she have of me?' 'What am I missing most in this relationship?' 'What are my core values and beliefs?' and the like.

Please write down the answers and reflect on them for a few days.

After a while, you will gain a better and more precise understanding of yourself and the boundaries you need in this relationship. You may discover that you value honesty the most and expect your children or partner to be more honest with you. You may find that you like to be alone with your friends and expect your partner to understand and respect that.

Please also think about how you feel about the other person in the relationship you are analyzing. Think about how this person makes you feel when he or she makes you feel or has ever made you feel insulted in any way, when he or she does something that makes you feel physically unsafe or uncomfortable, when he or she pressures you to do things that go against your values, when his or her demands overwhelm you, when he or she infantilizes you, or when he or she violates your sense of autonomy and control.

Some deep reflection will help you decide what boundaries you need to set with this person in order to move forward.

Once you have determined the boundaries you want in this relationship, it is time to communicate your needs to this person. You need to communicate effectively with them and avoid using poor wording, a rushed conversation, or vague requests.

It is best to come to the meeting prepared. Write down your points beforehand and review them so that you are clear about your expectations and needs.

Talk to the person when you know you are both relaxed. Let them know the agenda for the meeting and ask them if they are comfortable talking about it at the time you have specified. Sometimes the other person may try to back out by giving you various excuses for not being available. In this case, let them know that you will not move forward with the relationship unless they agree to discuss the issue off the record.

Try using more "I" statements instead of "you" when talking to the other person, as the latter can seem accusatory. For example, instead of saying, "You overwhelm me with your overbearing attitude," try saying, "I feel overwhelmed when I feel I do not have enough space to share my thoughts" (it is important to mention "that" way here).

Be as clear as you can about your needs and the boundaries you expect.

After you have spoken, ask the other person to express his or her feelings, concerns, and questions. Answer these concerns as calmly and clearly as you can. You do not need to justify your feelings or needs to them, but addressing their concerns will help them understand you better and respect the boundaries.

Also, ask your partner, parent, child, or whomever you are talking to about their needs and what kind of boundaries they expect you to follow. If you have certain expectations, they probably have some as well, and you both need to meet those needs and follow the appropriate boundaries.

After the discussion, encourage the other person to follow these boundaries. Make sure you follow through on the ones they asked you to work on.

Perhaps the person has become lax in practicing these boundaries. In that case, reiterate your needs and be very specific about the boundaries. Perhaps you were vague before and they did not properly understand your needs. Give this person the benefit of the doubt.

If the person continues to violate the boundaries, be firm again. Also, mention the consequences you may have to enforce if they continue to overstep your boundaries. For example, you might tell your partner that if he or she yells at you again, you may have to move out of the house for a while. Make sure that you only state the consequences that you will enforce so that they take you seriously.

Start working on these guidelines; if your loved ones really care about you, they will follow the boundaries you expect them to follow. In the same way, continue to work on all of your relationships.

There may be a case where a particular person with whom you wish to have a healthy relationship does not respect your boundaries. If they continue to ignore your feelings and continue the mistreatment you disapprove of, it is best to distance yourself from them.

It will take time, but if you are consistent, calm, and patient, you can establish healthy boundaries in your relationships. You can do it! Just be sure to reciprocate your loved one's efforts with more love, care, and respect.

If someone is willing to go the extra mile to improve their behavior for you, they love you. It is important to make them feel loved and cared for as well. I'm going to discuss some ways to really make that happen.

How to Express Trust, Love, Respect, and Care for Your Loved Ones

Love, care, respect, and trust are essential to keeping your relationships alive and happy.

A plant will wilt if you do not water it for a few days, right? Relationships are more or less the same. You must constantly feed them with love, affection, appreciation, respect, and trust to keep them thriving.

If your relationships are starting to get dull, here are some action steps to take:

Start by showing affection to your loved ones, especially your partner, children, parents, and siblings. Little things like, "I love you," "I know you work so hard to keep me happy and I want to be there for you," "You mean a lot to me," are often enough to do the trick.

Give some physical affection to relationships that crave it. Snuggle with your children, hug them often, and kiss them on the cheek. Hold your partner's hands, hug them from behind while they work, and give them a good hug to make them feel how much they mean to you.

When you meet your parents, hug them and feel their embrace for a while. Be sensitive to the other person's need for physical intimacy and affection. Some children do not like tight hugs, and some parents or friends have limits on physical contact, so be aware of that.

Make small gestures of love and kindness for your loved ones. Help your partner in the kitchen. You can fold laundry if they are in charge. Ask them if they need help with their chores or anything else. Similarly, help your children with their homework. Play with them more.

When it comes to friends, support them unconditionally. If someone needs emotional help, just be there and listen. If a friend needs financial help, see what you can do. Suppose you cannot help them with a second job or a better-paying opportunity. In that case, spend some time reflecting on your various relationships to see how you can better provide for them.

Inject lots and lots of trust into your relationships by giving them power, authority, and the discretion to think for themselves and make their own decisions. Of course, you must do this in a way that is appropriate to the nature of each relationship.

Remember that empowering your loved ones gives wings to your relationships and boosts your self-esteem. When it comes to your partner, trust her ability to make the right decisions and learn from her mistakes. For example, if your wife wants to experiment with digital marketing but you don't think it's a worthwhile skill, let her know that you trust and support her decision. Give her the confidence to think for herself.

As for your children, let them decide what to wear, what book to read (age appropriate), what to draw, and the like. If you have a teenager and they want to study a different course than you had in mind, let them do so.

Also, do not invade your loved one's privacy. Do not check your partner's phone or spy on who they are talking to. If you suspect that something naughty is going on in the relationship, whether with your partner or your children, speak up.

Whenever possible, give gifts to your loved ones. Surprise your boyfriend with his favorite pumpkin pie one day. Buy flowers for your girlfriend. Give your partner a briefcase or even a sweet love note. Gifts do not have to be expensive and extravagant. Little things given with love are more heartfelt, so be thoughtful and do something nice for them.

Spend quality time with your loved ones doing things you enjoy. Watch a movie with them, play in the park with them, draw with them, or let them choose the activity for the day.

Similarly, have a fun night out with your friends where you hang out, talk, or do something relaxing or fun together, such as a game of basketball. Keep date nights with your partner and make them the focus of your attention. Dedicate an hour each day to your partner, sharing your feelings, eating together, and enjoying each other's hugs.

If you can't do this every day, try to do it as often as possible throughout the week. Set aside a few days a month for your siblings and parents, if they live in the same city. See them, talk to them, and enjoy each other's company.

If you have been distant from a sibling or parent for a while, try to reach out to them. Accept your mistake where you are wrong, apologize, and ask them to work with you to improve the relationship. Consistency and love are the keys to mending broken hearts, and if you do it right, you can surely get your loved ones back.

These may seem like small things, but our small efforts for our loved ones speak volumes and bring them closer to you.

Your loved ones will return the gestures and efforts once you begin to make them. Keep expectations out of your relationships for a while, and just be there for your loved ones as genuinely as you can. Trust me, your efforts will yield great results.

Tips for Establishing Strong and Open Communication with Your Loved Ones

Open communication is essential to the growth of your relationships. But what is open communication?

Open communication is based on the principles of mindful, attentive listening and thoughtful speaking. Sharing your thoughts, feelings, fears, and hopes with your partner is important to keeping the relationship strong.

Discussing your children's ambitions, insecurities, doubts, and inner thoughts is important for them to feel heard. Asking your friends and siblings about their lives, problems, and aspirations is important to make them feel that you are there for them.

Talking to your parents often and allowing them to share their feelings, even their complaints, is an important way to make them feel that they can talk to you without hesitation.

At the same time, it is also important to share your thoughts, feelings, and aspirations with your loved ones, depending on the nature of the relationship.

Let me share with you some valuable tips for good and open communication with different loved ones.

Set aside time to talk with your partner without interruptions such as TV, cell phones, laptops, work commitments, children, etc. If you have children, it could be when they are less busy with activities, at school, or asleep. During this time, talk openly about how you feel about different things and ask them to do the same. If there is something urgent or important you want to discuss, let them know the agenda in advance so you don't surprise them with an important discussion.

Talk calmly about what is bothering you, and avoid using an accusatory tone.

If you have something to tell them, go first and let them know that you will listen patiently when it is their time to speak.

Be clear about your feelings and speak as politely as possible.

When discussing your aspirations, passion projects, or future endeavors, be explicit about what they mean to you. Talk about how certain things hold you back and how you want to feel free and relaxed.

Also share your feelings about them. Let them know the value they bring to your life, how much you love them, how serious you are about the relationship, and how much you want to have a beautiful life together.

When you are finished, encourage your spouse/boyfriend/girlfriend to share their feelings. Allow them to be as open as they feel comfortable. Listen patiently without fidgeting, using your phone, or breaking eye contact. This tip applies to communicating with anyone, including your children, friends, parents, siblings, coworkers, and boss.

If there is a conflict between you and your partner, try to find a middle ground. Let them know that you are willing to meet them halfway if they show the same level of understanding and compromise.

Also talk about financial matters, any secrets you want to share with your partner, and possibly anything else, including your fears and insecurities. If you feel they are being judgmental or closed-minded about something, ask them to discuss their feelings openly. At the same time, let them know that you need them to respect your feelings as well as theirs.

Also, be appreciative of your partner. Acknowledge and praise their strengths, beauty, charm, what you like about them, how much they do for you, and the like.

Allow your partner to be with you so that you can do the same.

Communicate with your children

Make it a point to talk to your children every day, even if it is only for 30 minutes. Ask them about their day at school, what they enjoyed most, what activities they like and don't like, what they want to do, and so on. Also ask them about any problems they are having at school, whether with a teacher or a classmate.

If you are homeschooling your child, ask them if they enjoy the curriculum and approach to teaching.

Encourage them to talk to you about their inhibitions and fears. If you and your partner have been strict with them lately, ask them what they would like to improve. Also, let them know what you expect from them.

With teenagers and older children, be open to discussing their ambitions and sexuality. Let them know that they are free to share anything with you, and even if you disapprove, you will respect it and not stand in their way. In this way, your children will gain confidence that you trust them and will be more willing to share things with you.

Also, appreciate and celebrate your children's small successes. If your child stops stuttering, take him or her out for a treat. If your daughter wins a debate contest, give her a nice gift. If your son has started to listen to you about making his bed and doing little chores by himself, give him a pat on the back and words of encouragement and appreciation.

Communicating with your parents

Always be respectful when communicating with your parents. Talk to them patiently and politely, and, avoid using harsh tones or rude words.

Share your life stories, events, and activities with them and ask them about theirs. Motivate and support them in their efforts if they want to pursue something.

For example, if your 65-year-old mother wants to start a pottery business, encourage her instead of telling her she is too old. If your parents didn't support your passions when you were younger, don't hold that against them and try to be supportive. In this way, you can teach them what a good support system looks like.

With controlling parents, let them know what you want to do and do not ask for advice. If they make suggestions and demand that you do things a certain way, be firm with them about your decision.

Communicating with Friends/Siblings

Be yourself with your friends and close siblings and encourage them to embrace their individuality.

Share anything you want to discuss with them in a positive way.

Joking around with friends, even your partner, is cool. However, if someone is offended by something you say, do not hesitate to apologize.

Respect, acceptance, and acknowledgement are important tools for communicating well with your loved ones.

The issue of consent

Consent is agreement or permission to do something. When a person consents to something, he or she is willing to engage in that activity alone or with you.

For any relationship to thrive, consent is a critical element. In the absence of consent, things can seem coercive and pressured. Therefore, make sure you get the other person's consent on every important and even trivial matter, because it may be important to them.

Consent is essential in all relationships, especially those you share with your partner. Get their consent if you are planning something with them, such as moving to a new neighborhood or city/country.

Also, get them comfortable with you first, and then make sure you have their consent in matters of intimacy. If you are starting a relationship with someone, try to hold their hands first and if they do not hesitate, move slowly. Take things slowly and make sure you get their permission before you do anything.

Ask your children's permission before enrolling them in anything. If you think your children might benefit from joining a swimming club, ask for their permission first. Similarly, if you know someone who might be a good match for your

20-year-old daughter, ask her if she would like to meet that person before arranging the meeting.

Similarly, ask your friends' permission before you plan something new with them, use something that belongs to them, or decide where you both will be involved. For example, if you and your friend run a business together, get their permission before outsourcing the marketing department to an agency.

When you begin to seek the approval of your loved ones, you begin to give them the confidence to believe in themselves and to feel comfortable around you.

Loving your loved ones truly and wholeheartedly takes a lot of effort, but it is extremely rewarding. When loved ones bring love into your life, you feel more fulfilled and empowered.

As you strengthen your relationships and your self-esteem, your life begins to gain a sense of balance and tranquility.

For that, you need to reclaim your power. Let's talk about this in the next chapter, "*Self-Esteem and Reclaiming Your Power.*"

Chapter 10: Self-Esteem & Reclaiming Your Power

"When you observe rather than react, you reclaim your power."

Denise Linn

We all have an inner personal power: a sense of control over our lives, actions, behaviors, and choices. This sense of power is critical to increasing your self-esteem and empowerment.

Let us better understand your personal power, how it affects your self-esteem, and how you can reclaim it.

What is Your Personal Power?

Your inner (personal) power is your ability to believe in yourself, trust your competence, and know that you can handle whatever lemons life throws your way because you will make lemonade out of them anyway.

Your power includes the following key elements:

Strong self-belief includes knowing your worth and having complete confidence in yourself despite your shortcomings. When you recognize and unleash your power, you become fearless because you become more aware of your rights and how best to use them.

Understand your rights and assert them when necessary: Instead of being bossed around by others, you become the sole boss of your life and can steer it in a direction that aligns with your beliefs, values, and sense of purpose. Assertiveness is about respectfully standing up for your rights and using your power to protect your rights without violating the rights of others.

Taking Responsibility: By unleashing your power, you take full responsibility for your life and actions and ensure that they are in harmony. You admit your mistakes and learn from them, making amends where necessary. As a result, you become a better version of yourself and feel better equipped to handle life's challenges.

You pursue your deepest and most authentic desires and realize your goals: You unleash your power and pursue your most authentic and meaningful needs and desires. Instead of falling for superficial desires, you figure out what you really want and pursue it.

Not only do you pursue it, but you begin to turn your dreams into reality. Your power also gives you the confidence to live your life with a sense of purpose and to do something worthwhile with your life, something that gives you meaning and pure joy.

So, your power is nothing less than a magical elixir that helps you transform your life into the one you have always wanted, so that you can completely reclaim it.

Now let us discover what you must do to unleash your inner potential and personal power.

Inner Power Lies in Unlocking Your Spirituality

As mentioned earlier, spirituality is finding meaning in your life. We all have a purpose to fulfill in our lives. We are in this universe to do something meaningful, but not many realize this.

We are usually busy with many things, but we often feel a void in our lives and don't feel connected to it. If this feeling resonates with you, you are probably missing the spiritual connection to yourself.

Spirituality brings great meaning to your life by helping you identify your purpose and encouraging you to pursue it. You find out what you are meant to do, even if it is just making art, starting a cleaning business, or raising healthy, confident children.

Your purpose can be anything, but once you identify it and align your life with it, it automatically begins to ignite joy.

Let me tell you a story to illustrate this point.

President Kennedy visited the NASA space center in 1962. He saw a janitor and asked him what he was doing. The janitor's answer was simple but powerful. I am helping to put a man on the moon, Mr. President.

This profound answer made the president understand how this janitor knew his purpose and how he was adding value to something greater than his existence. As you can see from this story, when you understand your purpose, you do it with complete passion, commitment and sincerity, which increases the quality of your life.

How does spirituality unlock your power & increase your self-esteem?

Spirituality is about unlocking your spiritual self to understand the bigger picture beyond your physical reality. It helps you delve into the deeper aspects of your existence and the universe.

As you peel back the layers of your existence, you explore and understand your true needs. I mentioned how often we struggle with shiny object syndrome, people-pleasing behaviors, and other issues that make us settle for things we do not want or need.

We keep doing things, and many things may even bring us happiness, but it is always temporary. When the instant gratification wears off, we return to feeling disconnected and dismayed with our lives.

This problem changes for the better because when you understand and connect with your spiritual self, you are clear about your most genuine and authentic needs. You know what your life means to you, and you have clarity about how to best live it.

With all this information, you automatically feel more confident, and your self-esteem continues to blossom. Instead of falling prey to distractions, meaningless temptations, and superficial desires, you focus on what is important to you and embrace your individuality. You feel complete in your existence and use it to add value to the universe. As a result, you constantly increase your self-esteem.

Now that you know how your spirituality can help you increase your self-esteem, let us talk about what can help you unleash it along with your power.

Spend some time thinking about who you are and what your existence means to you.

Ask yourself questions such as: 'Why am I here?' 'What would I do if I didn't have time, money, and energy constraints?' 'What do I thrive on?' 'What do I need to survive and thrive in this world?' 'What are my highest needs?' 'What does my heart and soul desire?' 'What do I feel connected to?' 'What is my true passion (or passions)?

What can I do all the time without getting tired?' 'What does my life mean to me?' 'What does this universe mean to me?' 'Is there a purpose to my existence?' 'How do I add value to this universe?' and the like.

As you reflect on one question, many similar questions will arise.

Take the time to explore every aspect of a question and write down the answers in detail.

Make it a point to spend at least 10 to 15 minutes each day thinking about your spirituality and your power.

Soon different answers will come to you that will help you align your existence with your spirituality and this universe. While you are working on this, you need to start working on the next activity. The answers to these practices will help you to identify your clear and meaningful goals and add tremendous value to your life.

Exploring Your True Potential

Your true potential helps you gain greater clarity about your sense of purpose. When you know what you are exceptionally talented at, you can use that knowledge and awareness to effectively use your time and make the most of your existence.

To find out, here's what you need to do:

If you have been working in a particular industry for some time, you may have developed one or more skills. Write that down. For example, if you have been teaching for half a decade and are good at teaching young children, write that down in your journal.

If you haven't started your career yet, think about a career you want to pursue and the skills you need to learn. For example, if working in a marketing firm sounds appealing, you need to learn marketing.

Next, think of something you like to do, think about, and talk about. It can be anything, such as fashion, food, fitness, anime, aesthetics, cars, gadgets, motivation, gardening, soccer, etc. Write down your findings. If there is more than one thing, write them down and then arrange them in descending order, from the one you are most passionate about to the one you are least passionate about.

Then think of one thing that people, especially strangers, often compliment you on. When strangers praise someone, they do so openly and without bias, so the compliment is likely to be honest and authentic.

Write down what you receive compliments on in relation to your skills and character traits. For example, if you get compliments on your good communication skills and soothing voice, add those to the list.

Consider your interests and preferences. What are the things you like to do? These activities are different from your passion, because your passion is something you never get bored or annoyed by. Usually people are passionate about one or a few things, but they can have multiple interests and likes.

Once you have jotted down all these points, you need to find a nexus point to determine your true potential and purpose. Yes, this requires you to think deeply, ask many relevant questions, and take time.

It takes weeks to months for people to realize their sense of purpose and hidden potential. So do not rush the process. After your introspection, you may find that you have accounting skills, like to talk, are passionate about educating people, and have a clear, strong voice. Perhaps your purpose could be to educate people about setting up their accounts and spreading awareness about accounting-related topics and issues.

Once you have identified your purpose and true potential, see how you feel about it. Write this down in your journal and revisit it every 2 to 3 days. You may feel that you have two or three purposes. Think about each one and choose the one you feel most connected to.

Now you need to explore it further and create a plan and goals to actualize it.

Plan to Actualize Your Purpose to Unleash Your Inner Power

Imagine the powerful sense of accomplishment and fulfillment you will experience when you begin to live your life with purpose. When you know what your heart wants and wake up each day feeling energized to move closer to your purpose, you have discovered your inner power.

With a great sense of power and purpose, your self-esteem will be quite high.

So here's what you need to do to get to that level:

Write down your purpose again on a new page in your journal.

Think about where you see yourself in ten years. Write that down. Continuing with the example of creating awareness of accounting issues, perhaps you see yourself opening a chain of institutes that provide accounting and finance-related consulting and teach people various skills related to the two subjects.

Imagine yourself in that position. If it lights a spark in your heart and makes you feel emotionally charged, it is probably what you should pursue. Tune into your gut and listen carefully. Our gut is often true and leads us to something meaningful, so do not ignore it.

Once you have clarity on your 10-year goal, break it down into two 5-year goals. For example, in this case, your 5-year goal might be to have an accounting practice that generates $50,000 a month for you.

Again, spend some time thinking about your 5-year goal to make sure you are clear on it and have a goal that means something to you and one that you would not give up on come what may.

Make your 5-year goal a SMART goal. SMART is a tool for creating powerful goals that are incredibly clear and help you get started. SMART stands for specific, measurable, attainable, realistic, and time-bound, which means these elements must be a core part of any goal you want to achieve.

Take your 5-year goal and make it a SMART GOAL.

First, make it specific. Think about what specific thing you want to accomplish in 5 years. If you want to make money from it, how much will that be? Vague goals only create confusion and prevent the universe from supporting you properly.

The Universe operates on the principle of the Law of Attraction, which means 'like attracts like'. Whatever you put out into the universe in terms of your thoughts, beliefs, and actions, the universe will send you similar things, experiences, ideas, vibes, people, and opportunities.

With vague goals like 'I want more money,' 'I want to start a business,' and 'I want to be successful,' you confuse the universe about what to send you. When your goals are specific, you are thinking exactly along those lines, signaling to the Universe the experiences you want to send your way. So, make sure your goal is as specific and clear as possible.

Next, you must make it measurable. To achieve a goal, you must measure your performance against it. If your goal isn't measurable, it won't be easy to achieve because you won't know how to evaluate and track your performance. In this case, you can measure the success of your institution by the revenue and profit it generates.

Third, your goal must be attainable. Achievable goals can be accomplished with your current resources. For example, if you want to learn to play the piano but do not have the funds to enroll in a music school or take specialized piano lessons, you could buy a used piano and learn from YouTube tutorials and free online courses, or perhaps you could ask an expert piano player to mentor you.

As for a 5-year goal, you cannot estimate the resources you will have in 5 years because things and life are constantly evolving. However, you can write down the resources you are likely to need to accomplish the goal, and then use the resources you have now to get started on the goal.

For example, if you want to open an accounting institute, you may not have the resources to do so right away, but you can start with the most basic step of the process: creating awareness. How would you do that? You could create a blog, a YouTube channel, social media pages, etc. For now, this is how you make the goal attainable. The achievability element is especially important for short-term goals and weekly milestones.

Fourth, your goals must be realistic. When you imagine your purpose and think of your vision, it can be as big as you want. For example, imagining a business empire worth billions of dollars is totally cool.

Breaking it down into goals has to be realistic so you believe it is true and start working on it. If a goal seems unrealistic, it is likely to overwhelm you and keep your mind from working on it. When you set your 5-year goal, keep it realistic so that you will work on it seriously.

Finally, your goal needs to be time-bound, so it should have a time frame and a deadline. Goals without deadlines become vague and lose their value. If you don't know when a project is due, you're likely to procrastinate, thinking you have plenty of time.

But with a deadline and a clear timeframe, you know when to start and when each milestone is due. Set a deadline to make your 5-year goal time-bound; this applies to any goal you set.

Once you have your 5 Year Goal, you need to make it more manageable and actionable. Thinking about a big 5-year goal can also be overwhelming and demotivating, especially if you have struggled with self-esteem issues.

To overcome this problem, break it down into five 1-year goals, and then work on each 1-year goal individually. For example, if you want to open an accounting institute, your first 1-year goal could be to have your own YouTube channel with over 50,000 followers. This means that your audience is listening to you and is likely to follow your recommendations. Based on this 1-year goal, create a SMART goal. Make sure it is specific, measurable, attainable, realistic, and time-bound.

Next, take that 1-year goal and break it down into 4 to 6 3- or 2-month milestones. To do this, ask yourself what you need to do to achieve this 1-year goal. Write down the answers. These steps or tasks will help you create your detailed action plan.

For example, for your YouTube channel, you would need a name, content for the videos, video editing, some graphic design, YouTube optimization, monetization strategy, and the like. Everything you need is a task in itself. If you take each task and start thinking about what you need to get it done, you will come up with bite-sized steps that detail what you need to do to get it done.

Review your available resources to analyze whether you can outsource help for any of these tasks. Delegating your work will help you manage it better. However, if you are strapped for cash, it is okay to go slow and do things yourself for a while.

Once you have completed each step, create a 1-year, monthly, and weekly plan. It should include daily and weekly goals with corresponding to-do items. Each milestone should also have its "priority status" and a deadline.

Go over your action plan a few times to make sure it is as foolproof as possible. It's okay to make a few mistakes and have room for improvement, so don't be too hard on yourself if you make some mistakes.

Once you have your action plan in place, you need to start following it. I have already shared time management hacks that you can use to implement your action plan.

Another important tip is to review your goal and visualize yourself achieving it. Supplement this with positive affirmations based on your purpose and goals and you will gradually move towards it.

Unleash your inner creativity

Each of us has unimaginable creative abilities. It is only a matter of tapping into them to unleash them and use them to maximize our inner power.

Being creative does not mean being involved in some form of art. It is about creating unique solutions to your problems, thinking outside the box, experimenting with new ideas, putting a fresh spin on existing ideas, and trying to leave your mark in everything you do.

When you think and work more creatively in every aspect of your life, you begin to think optimistically and feel more in control. You feel like you can handle anything, which is how you sharpen your power.

So how do you become more creative?

Try different things

Experimenting with different ideas and trying new things is one of the best ways to tap into your creative abilities. When you try new things, new connections are made in your brain, improving your cognition and intelligence. You think more clearly and come up with new ideas.

You may not think this is directly related to pursuing your goals, but it is directly related to everything you do. Experimentation makes you see the same situation differently and helps you think better with a fresh perspective.

Here are a few things you might try:

Pick a new activity every two weeks and do it. For example, if you have never hiked, try it with friends. If you have never done pottery, take a class. Try learning to play an instrument. Any new experience may feel a little uncomfortable, but it will make you feel more courageous, which will help build your power.

Try doing routine things differently. For example, if you usually drink a cappuccino in the morning, try a latte. If you don't eat cereal for breakfast, try it one morning. Walk to work one day (if it is close) instead of taking a cab. These things may seem small, but they allow you to have different experiences that diversify your thinking capacity.

Think mindfully, with an open and accepting mind, whenever you want to put a creative spin on something. Consider how a child would approach the situation or how someone from a different generation would handle it. As you nudge your mind to think differently, it begins to follow your direction.

Spend time in nature

Spend some time each week in nature. Take a walk in the woods, watch the trees, hang out on the beach, watch a sunset, and try things like that.

Nature has a very calming effect on our minds and bodies. With a relaxed body and calm mind, you will feel more energetic and begin to cultivate the ability to think more creatively.

Approach your action plan differently

Analyze your action plan and the steps you have listed.

Think about how you can execute each step for maximum results. For example, if you want to reach more people to raise awareness about animal rights, you may want to organize a small meeting in your community instead of just making flyers and handing them out. A meeting will give you a chance to meet some people in person, and even if two people become interested in your work, that is better than handing out 100 flyers and getting no response.

Read a lot

Read and read some more, because as Dr. Seuss once said, "The more you read, the more you know. The more you know, the more places you'll go. Reading broadens your horizons and opens your mind to new ideas and concepts that will help you strategize better and become a smarter version of yourself.

When you read, don't just stick to things you like. Instead, read about every subject and topic you can find. Read fiction, politics, science, fitness, sports, fashion, etc. You never know when or where you'll find interesting inspiration to help you create unique solutions to your problems.

Make sure you write down or record the different strategies you try to become more creative and the ideas you come up with.

You will find yourself full of enthusiasm and optimism with each passing day. There is one more thing you need to work on to unleash your inner strength: by becoming more resilient, you will develop greater grit.

Build Resilience and Grit for Lasting Self-Esteem

Resilience is about staying strong in the face of adversity and your ability to bounce back to your goal or purpose after going through a challenging situation that makes you feel like you have failed. Conversely, grit is about sustained and consistent effort toward your goals, even after periodic setbacks.

Research shows that grit is one of the most important character traits you need to be successful-no matter how you define success.

Grit-consistently moving toward your goals-requires resilience. How is this important to unlocking your inner power?

Your inner power is directly related to your belief in yourself, your sense of fulfillment and accomplishment, and your ability to do what your heart truly wants. Resilience helps you with all of this because when you are resilient, setbacks do not scare you. You understand that they are temporary and that after a hiccup, you have to get back on track.

Instead of wallowing in misery, you bounce back and work to improve. As a result, you become more resilient and continue to work toward your goals, even when hell breaks loose.

Here's how to build resilience and grit:

Embrace challenges: First, reframe how you perceive them; every time you experience a challenge, you probably see it as negative. Instead of seeing it that way, think of it as your friend trying to help you get better. I know it is hard to think this way at first, but with the help of positive affirmations and creative visualizations, you can begin to befriend your challenges as well.

Whenever you get stuck in a rut, say to yourself, "This is temporary, and it is here to help me. What is it trying to tell me about my problem? How can I handle it better? Then give yourself positive affirmations such as, "I can do this," "This is a fairly easy situation to handle," "I am strong and resilient," and the like. After a few weeks, you will find it easy to stay calm when unpleasant situations knock on your door.

Understand that failure isn't bad: Wrap your head around the idea that failure is never bad. Failure helps you better understand your mistakes and what not to do. Maybe you ran a social media campaign to spread awareness about animal rights, but it did not go well. Review it and look at the words you used, the ad copy for it, the visuals, and other similar aspects. You will probably find the problem; the next time you run a campaign, you will know what not to do.

Don't stand still for long: Whenever you encounter a difficulty, you are likely to shut down for a while. It is natural to feel dismayed and want to do nothing. That's okay. But don't let this feeling last too long. Slowing down for a day or two is okay, but force yourself to jump back up and tackle the problem on the third day. Revisiting your goals and chanting affirmations can help you keep the big picture in mind and move toward it.

Feed your mind positive mental food: Just as our food affects our health, the things we read and listen to are like mental food for our minds. You need a lot of positive mental food to keep your mind strong and positive. Listen to TED Talks by accomplished, gritty people, read books on goal setting, motivation, and resilience, and spend time with positive, courageous people so that you continue to train your mind to think about resilience and grit.

It is only a matter of time before you start working on your goals with newfound resilience and grit. I am sure that your inner power will help you to emerge victorious, to fulfill your purpose of helping the homeless and orphans, or to create a chain of organic grocery stores.

Our self-esteem journey is coming to an end. So far, you have learned a lot about self-improvement and self-esteem. Now all you need to do is monitor your progress and continue to grow with each passing day.

The final chapter of the book, "Monitoring Your Progress and Continuing to Grow," covers this topic.

Chapter 11: Monitor Your Progress and Continue to Grow

"Personal growth is about progress, not perfection."

Hal Elrod

Growth comes from continually learning and continuing your journey toward your purpose. Achieving progress requires that you monitor your progress, adopt an attitude of learning and improving, and let go of past pain in order to move forward gracefully.

We all know that life can be difficult and tough at times. When things go haywire, undesirable situations keep popping up, and you cannot get the results you want, it is easy to lose your cool. But the truth is that this is life.

You must understand that nothing is permanent; this too will pass. If the good times weren't permanent, the bad times can't be permanent either. Instead of worrying about the duration of a hardship, focus more on moving forward, and here's the best way to do it.

Adopt a learning attitude

Work on developing a mindset of learning new things, unlearning old concepts and habits, and learning from wherever you can to improve yourself and achieve constant growth. This shift in perspective is what the growth mindset is all about, right?

Here is a list of important guidelines for you to follow:

Every time you come across a new concept, a different way to handle a situation, or a new spin on an old idea, don't dismiss it. Instead, write it down, take a picture if you can, and think about it more deeply when you are alone. Think about what it is trying to teach you and use that learning in your life.

Never stop a child or someone younger than you from teaching you something. If your son tells you about an app that you think is useless, listen with an open mind. It may be what you need for your business, or it may give you an idea for an app.

Listen to any criticism in a very positive way, just as we learned earlier. Take a deep breath and remember how the criticism will help you. Even if you ignore it, acknowledge that you have listened to the criticism and are becoming more open to it. Small gestures of self-appreciation will boost your self-esteem and help you become more confident.

Spend five minutes a day researching the latest trends, world events, new applications, technological advances, and the like; this will help you learn more about how the world works and encourage you to step up your game.

If you follow these guidelines, you will be amazed at how much you will begin to learn and how easy it will be for you to grow.

Monitor your progress

Monitoring your progress is the best way to get better every day. It helps you identify your mistakes, recognize your strengths, celebrate your milestones, and move up a rung on the "success" ladder.

To track your progress, try this strategy:

At the end of each day, review what you did with an open and accepting mind.

See if you accomplished any of your goals. If you did, give yourself credit and analyze your action strategy.

Also, see if you missed any deadlines or failed to complete any tasks. Ask yourself why this happened and develop ways to address the issues the next day instead of beating yourself up about it.

Write down your progress along with the milestones you reached and the deadlines you missed, and see if you need to change your action plan and the deadlines associated with each task.

Evaluate your various experiences throughout the day and how they affected your mood, behavior, and productivity. Perhaps you received negative feedback from one of your clients that dampened your spirits. Once you felt demotivated, you couldn't work on other tasks. Instead of this situation, you need to improve your ability to handle negative feedback and take it positively.

Second, you must improve your performance so that such instances do not occur again. Third, you need to encourage yourself to work on other tasks, even if one does not go as planned.

You can also create performance charts and review them regularly to keep track.

Forgive yourself, heal past wounds, and move on

One of the biggest obstacles to working on our goals is not being able to forgive ourselves for our past mistakes and allowing past wounds to bother us.

For example, you may be creating a plan for your gardening blog and get stuck trying to publish a new post; this may remind you of when you couldn't learn to drive and almost crashed the car during a driving lesson. Our minds have a strange way of bringing up memories, sometimes unrelated ones.

Whenever this happens, you will probably stop and not move at all. Do not let this happen over and over again. Instead, train yourself to keep moving.

Here's what you need to do:

Every few days, sit quietly with yourself and think about your past mistakes, especially the ones you haven't forgiven yourself for.

Write them down and how you still feel about them.

237

Take a deep breath and say, "I choose to forgive myself and move on.

As you say this, burn the piece of paper. As it crumbles to ashes, imagine all the pain and hurt seeping out of your body, mind, and soul.

Say, 'I am relaxed and ready to move forward in life.

Make this a weekly practice and soon your past wounds will stop hurting all the time. They may still come to you as fleeting memories, but you won't allow them to disturb your peace of mind.

Whenever you make a mistake, tell yourself, "It's okay. Let's think about how we can fix it and do better. This kind of suggestion lifts your spirits and allows you to move on in life, focusing more on the solution than the problem.

As you begin to forgive yourself and treat yourself with more kindness, you will easily move on from all the pain you have felt in the past and allow peace to reside within you.

Conclusion

Well, here you are. You have completed this guide to increasing your self-esteem.

Reading this book proves your commitment to empowering, enhancing and strengthening your self-esteem. This is the spirit you need to live the rest and best of your life with grace.

I am incredibly grateful to you for embarking on this journey because you are helping yourself (and your friends, family, and business relationships) fulfill a higher purpose.

One of the greatest feelings on this journey is empowering people to feel the highest joy in life and love. It is about learning to live better. I hope this guide stays with you and continues to help you.

I believe in you and that you are capable of doing great things in this world. The magic of this gift is that it works when you practice it. From this day forward, I want you to practice connecting with your higher self.

Be good to yourself at all times and speak to your subconscious in a new frame of mind and voice. Begin today to build a relationship with who you really are and who you are meant to be.

The only way through the gates to a life of joy and fulfillment is the willingness to step outside of who you are to become who you want to be. Start acting like this new person now, and your future self will thank you.

And I thank you for investing in yourself, your journey, and your future. There are greater things to come, and you are worthy of all the things you dream of.

Until next time, my friends...

Scott Allan

"The secret to self-confidence isn't to stop caring what people think; it's to start caring about what you think. It's to make your opinion of you more important than anyone else's."

About Scott Allan

Scott Allan is an international bestselling author of over 30 books published in 12 languages in the area of personal growth and self-development. He is the author of **Fail Big**, **Undefeated,** and **Do the Hard Things First**.

As a former corporate business trainer in Japan, and **Transformational Mindset Strategist**, Scott has invested over 10,000 hours of research and instructional coaching into the areas of self-mastery and leadership training.

With an unrelenting passion for teaching, building critical life skills, and inspiring people around the world to take charge of their lives, Scott Allan is committed to a path of **constant and never-ending self-improvement**.

Many of the success strategies and self-empowerment material that is reinventing lives around the world evolves from Scott Allan's 20 years of practice and teaching critical skills to corporate executives, individuals, and business owners.

You can connect with Scott at:

scottallan@scottallanpublishing.com

www.scottallanbooks.com

Scott Allan

"Master Your Life One Book at a Time."

<u>Subscribe</u> to the weekly newsletter for actionable
content and updates on future book releases from
Scott Allan

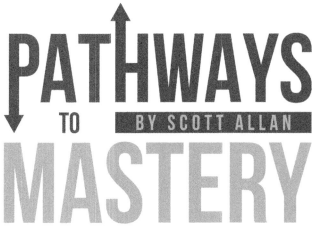

PATHWAYS
TO
BY SCOTT ALLAN
MASTERY
THE SERIES

Made in the USA
Las Vegas, NV
17 January 2024

84501903R00152